Skillstreaming
in Early Childhood

REVISED EDITION

New Strategies and Perspectives for Teaching Prosocial Skills

Ellen McGinnis
Arnold P. Goldstein

● ●

Research Press
2612 North Mattis Avenue • Champaign, Illinois 61822
(800) 519-2707 • www.researchpress.com

Composition by Jeff Helgesen
Cover design by Linda Brown, Positive I.D. Graphic Design, Inc.
Printed by Bang Printing

ISBN 0–87822–449–1
Library of Congress Control Number 2002111197

*To Sara Kathleen Smith—may this be of help to you
in your career of teaching young children. The opportunity
to make a difference is yours.
—E. M.*

*To Lauren and Rachel,
with love and admiration
—A. P. G.*

CONTENTS

FIGURES AND TABLES

FIGURES

TABLES

PREFACE

We have within our reach a tremendous opportunity to change the problematic behaviors of the young child, before these behaviors become well-established patterns that create significant stress for the child, teachers, parents, and others in the child's world. When parents and educators work together, the impact for the preschool and kindergarten child is far reaching and long lasting. Skillstreaming is a prescriptive instructional intervention designed to teach prosocial behavioral alternatives to children and youth. This book addresses the implementation of this strategy with the preschool and kindergarten child, emphasizing the importance of family involvement in this endeavor. Although the focus is on children ages 3 through 6, the Skillstreaming strategy and the 40 skills included in this volume are also appropriate for many children in the early primary grades (grades 1 and 2) who lack the maturity to benefit from more complex skills instruction (i.e., *Skillstreaming the Elementary School Child,* McGinnis & Goldstein, 1997).

Skillstreaming is now used in hundreds of schools, day care settings, agencies, and residential centers serving youth throughout the United States and beyond. Introduced in 1976 as one of the first social skills instruction approaches for adults and adolescents, this method has been used successfully in settings serving preschool and elementary school children. Skillstreaming, which first began in isolated classrooms with small groups of children, has continued to find greater use in general education on a schoolwide and districtwide basis.

The purpose of this revised edition is to share with teachers and others (mental health professionals, child care workers, counselors) what has been learned about Skillstreaming with preschool children during the past decade. How does this revised edition differ from the original *Skillstreaming in Early Childhood* (McGinnis & Goldstein, 1990)? The teaching methods and specific skills, validated by research conducted over many years and with many different populations, remain the same. The revision presents the most current information related to the program's use with young children—information derived from its hands-on application by many hundreds of teachers and youth care workers—as well as our own experiences during the decades since the program's inception.

We begin by introducing Skillstreaming in an educational and developmental context related directly to children (chapter 1). The past history and development of Skillstreaming, as well as its current and future directions with children who exhibit difficult behaviors—including behaviors such as aggression and bullying—are discussed in chapter 2. Instructional arrangements (e.g., physical setting, time for instruction, skills agenda) for implementing Skillstreaming (chapter 3) and current teaching procedures (chapter 4) are presented in a detailed and user-friendly manner. Direct teaching procedures are illustrated by presenting a transcript of a Skillstreaming group with children at the kindergarten level (chapter 5). Chapter 6 presents the 40 skills for instruction, giving each skill's behavioral steps, teacher notes to enhance the effectiveness of instruction, and suggested topics for modeling displays. Due to the contextual nature of social behaviors, additional considerations to refine and perfect skill performance are provided in chapter 7. The serious challenge of generalization of learned skills (chapter 8) and interventions to deal effectively with problematic behaviors that occur in the instructional setting (chapter 9) are discussed. A rationale and strategies for involving parents in this very important work are addressed in chapter 10.

Five appendixes respectively present (a) an annotated bibliography of Skillstreaming research related to children and adolescents, (b) copies of the Skillstreaming checklists and grouping chart, (c) a rubric for assessing skill competence in children, (d) a description of supplementary Skillstreaming materials at the preschool and primary levels (including Skill Cards and a Program Forms book), and (e) a list of Skillstreaming materials for other instructional levels.

ACKNOWLEDGMENTS

Two very special people provided impetus for both the original work of *Skillstreaming in Early Childhood* (McGinnis & Goldstein, 1990) and this revision. First, thank you to Alex Smith, who was a preschooler at the time of the original text and who provided many opportunities for me to apply this strategy as a parent. He has become a wonderful young person who continues to provide warm encouragement and reinforcement, always with a combination of reflection and humor. Second, thank you to Sara Smith, who is an intuitive, talented, and kind young woman who is working toward becoming a teacher of young children. She has provided the motivation for this text revision, which has truly been a labor of love.

Thank you also to our publisher, Ann Wendel, for her ongoing support and for the friendship we have developed through this venture as well as through other opportunities and challenges. This friendship is a reminder of what is truly valuable.

—E. M.

CHAPTER 1
Introduction

Growing up in today's world, young children require more support than ever before. School, family, and community violence continue to be pervasive concerns. The stress on today's changing families often places more responsibility on children to seek support outside the family. As a result of financial necessity, public schools are often merging, resulting in larger, potentially less personal learning settings. Those who teach and work with young children continue to look for ways to provide support in responding to the effects of these societal changes as well as to address the very different environmental demands children experience as they enter the world of school.

An increasing number of children who enter the doors of preschools and kindergarten classrooms lack the basic social skills to interact positively with others, to solve problems, to follow directions, and to participate in preacademic, academic and social learning. Some children are lonely and respond by isolating themselves from their peers. Others display high levels of acting-out and aggressive behavior. Still others have difficulty following simple directions due to their inability to attend. Consider the following real-life scenarios:

> At recess time, Cory, age 6, is often viewed by his kindergarten teacher on the sidelines of a group. He often stands by himself and watches the ongoing play, not making any attempt to join in the activity. The teacher has encouraged Cory many times to play with the others and has even talked with him about what games he likes to play at recess, but Cory continues to be just an observer. His teacher feels discouraged.

> In one preschool classroom, Juan and Elizabeth, age 4, both want all the Legos, even though there are enough to share. Elizabeth shouts out that all the Legos are hers and

1

tells Juan to get away. Juan replies no and continues to build his Lego tower. Elizabeth angrily scoops away many of the Legos, pushes Juan on the shoulder, and knocks down his tower. The teacher feels frustrated and tells Elizabeth that she must take a time-out.

Latecia, age 6, often gets in trouble for playing with little trinkets she keeps in her desk. When her first-grade teacher gives directions, Latecia rarely knows what she has been asked to do. Occasionally, Latecia will look at what another child is doing in an attempt to figure out what she should be working on. Very soon, however, she is engaged with another distraction. Latecia's teacher is annoyed.

Rami, age 6, appears to enjoy working by himself at the classroom learning center. One of his classmates wanders past the center where Rami is working and brushes against him. Rami turns and shouts at the peer, "You hit me! You wanna fight?" Most of the children in the class stop what they are doing and look toward the boys. The teacher stops working with other students and intervenes. Rami often seems to attribute negative motivations to his peers, and the class is often disrupted by his outbursts. His teacher feels hopeless to help him.

What Cory, Elizabeth, Latecia, and Rami lack, or are weak in, are the skills, abilities, or behaviors needed to interact with others in appropriate ways; to react prosocially to common, everyday stressors; or to exhibit the school-related behaviors necessary to benefit from preacademic instruction. In other words, these children are deficient in prosocial skills, just as low achievers are deficient in academic readiness or academic skills. Children may not have acquired the specific skills needed, or they may not be able to perform the skills adequately. Others may lack the fluency and flexibility of skill use to be socially competent in their interactions with others. Some children may misperceive the intent of others' actions, words, or nonverbal behaviors. Still others may be able to react in prosocial ways under some circumstances but fail to perform in desirable ways when prosocial skill use is most critical.

Although many educational interventions have focused on decreasing undesirable social behaviors, educators and others have become increasingly aware that doing so is insufficient to bring about desired behavioral change. Furthermore, when such interventions to decrease undesirable behaviors are the only ones employed, children are often left even lonelier and more rejected and socially isolated. The recommended alternative is to engage in planned instruction and skill-focused strategies to actually teach young children behaviors that are acceptable and rewarding, and that facilitate good interpersonal relationships and readiness to achieve academically.

THE PRESCHOOL AND KINDERGARTEN CHILD

By age 3, the age typically denoting the end of toddlerhood and the beginning of the preschool years, most young children are beginning to view themselves as part of a larger world—a world including demands that implicit and explicit skill competencies be mastered if the important adults in that world are to be pleased. Piaget (1962) has termed the ages between 2 and 7 the *preoperational stage,* a time when children begin to contemplate their actions and become increasingly aware of how their behavior brings about either desired rewards—such as smiles, hugs, or words of praise—or undesired punishments—such as frowns, reprimands, or loss of privileges.

Allen and Marotz (2000) describe how language, cognitive skills, and social behavior of young children develop at various ages. During the preschool years, there is great change in all areas of the child's development. The child's verbal and cognitive skills develop rapidly, thus enabling the child to develop some control over his or her own behavior, to solve problems, and to express ideas verbally. During these years, the child is also making the transition from parallel play, in which the child engages in independent play while a peer does likewise, to more interactive and cooperative play. The child is also beginning to develop a sense of the needs of others (empathy), to cooperate, and to plan ahead. From kindergarten age (ages 5 and 6) through age 8, more formal school routines are required, and the child acquires a strong interest in pleasing others and doing things right. Social interactions become more frequent and complex (Hartup, 1983), and friendships become increasingly more important.

TEACHING PROSOCIAL SKILLS

Why need we be concerned with social skills deficits at this early age? One central reason for teaching prosocial skills to young children concerns the new demands placed on them by the preschool and kindergarten settings. With this important change, children must all at once learn to get along not only with one or two siblings or neighborhood friends, but also with an entire classroom of other children and adults. Along with this increased social interaction comes the need for the child to acquire a new set of skills.

Also at this time, quite abruptly, adult and group demands become far greater and more complex. The child is now required to direct attention to an other-selected activity, to sit among a group of other children in close proximity, to change activities according to an adult time frame, to follow a variety of instructions, and to interact cooperatively with other children across a changing variety of tasks and settings. Such demands are not typically included in the home environment in such a structured and consistent manner. Therefore, the young child's first encounter with preschool or kindergarten typically involves an array of foreign skills and behaviors.

In this regard, Chan and Rueda (1979) describe a "hidden curriculum" operating within schools. This curriculum involves the assumption that all children enter the school setting with similar experiences and values. In other words, it is expected that children will have developed certain language and cognitive skills by exploring their environments and that they will have acquired a set of student behaviors enabling them to respond appropriately to adult instructions. This assumption appears to be faulty. Instead, teachers of young children encounter a diverse group of individuals having very different personalities and temperamental characteristics (Keogh & Burnstein, 1988), some who have had prior day care or preschool experiences and some who are entering a structured school setting for the first time. The cognitive and behavioral skills of children with less school-related experience may not be sufficient to meet the needs of the new, in-school situation.

Social skills deficits have also been the target of considerable research scrutiny, and it is well accepted today that a child's lack of social competence relates to his or her later adjustment. Mize (1995) notes that "children who experience trouble in peer interaction during preschool are at increased risk for academic difficulties and peer rejection or neglect in elementary school" (p. 238). A recent Surgeon General's report, the first of its kind, was undertaken in response to the Columbine High School tragedy, which occurred in April of 1999 (Youth Violence, 2001). A major finding in this report is that, for one of the two groups of youth who become violent, the violence begins before the age of puberty (generally prior to age 13). Members of this group "commit more crimes, and generally more serious crimes, for a longer time. These young people exhibit a pattern of escalating violence through childhood, and they sometimes continue their violence into adulthood" (introduction, p. 9). This report also notes, and it is important to emphasize here, that most children who are highly aggressive or who have been identified with a behavioral disorder do not later engage in violent acts; thus children who later become violent cannot be identified in early childhood and, clearly, the multiple factors likely to contribute to such an outcome are complex. Nonetheless, a major conclusion of this report is that "early childhood programs that target at-risk children and families are critical for preventing the onset of a chronic violent career" (introduction, p. 9).

What about members of the other group, who engage in serious violence during the teenage years? It appears that these youth do not give prior indication, either through a pattern of problematic behaviors or a high level of aggression, that they will become violent. Therefore, as this report concludes, "Targeting prevention programs solely to young children with problem behavior misses over half of the children who will eventually become serious violent offenders, although universal prevention programs in childhood may be effective in preventing late onset (youth) violence" (chapter 3, p. 2). Instruction in prosocial skill use is considered to be an important component of such violence prevention programs.

It appears clear that even very young children can benefit from instruction in prosocial skills. In their work with preschoolers and kindergarten children, Spivack and Shure (1974) found that 4- and 5-year-olds can be successfully taught to identify alternative problem solutions, anticipate consequences, and use other problem-solving skills that enhance interpersonal adjustment. Young children are also able to recognize more subtle aspects of social interactions. Ladd, Kochenderfer, and Coleman (2000), for example, in their study of kindergarten boys and girls, found that children of this age are able to recognize differences in quality of friendships. According to Maccoby (1980), these early years are the most critical for developing such prosocial behaviors as self-control and for organizing actions to achieve an external goal.

REMEDIATION AND PREVENTION

Skillstreaming is an approach toward remediating social skills deficits for a wide range of children. The child with an identified attention deficit disorder, for example, may have a particular need to learn the skills of Ignoring (Skill 8), Following Directions (Skill 10), and Interrupting (Skill 12) to better adapt to the structure of the classroom. The child with a learning disability may need to learn the skill of Asking for Help (Skill 6), as well as skills to deal with frustration, such as Trying When It's Hard (Skill 11), to facilitate preacademic and academic learning. Another child may misperceive the intent of peers' actions and would benefit from skills such as Reading Others (Skill 14) and Deciding How Someone Feels (Skill 25). Children with more severe disabilities, those with autism or mental disabilities, can be taught a variety of social skills to enhance their independence and to make their lives more satisfying. Those with emotional or behavioral disorders—whether characterized by withdrawal, aggression, or immaturity—need to learn prosocial skills as well. Although aggression and violence are very visible and perhaps cause more stress for peers, teachers, school administrators, parents, and the community, teaching prosocial skills to the withdrawn child or the child who reacts immaturely or inadequately is also important. Although many such children may not direct the distress of their social isolation outward or become aggressive toward others, they may later direct their aggression toward themselves through self-destructive behaviors.

Skillstreaming is also intended for the general education population—students whose behavior is not significantly problematic yet who will increase their personal satisfaction and happiness by learning or improving upon prosocial skills. In an effort to prevent future interpersonal and academic problems, many preschool and kindergarten children may need help with the skills to form friendships, to participate in problem solving, to avoid distractions when engaged in learning activities, or to deal productively with day-to-day stress. It is our hope that such skill learning will assist children in developing resiliency to problems that may occur at a later age.

WHAT IS SKILLSTREAMING?

Skillstreaming is a process that focuses on four direct instruction principles of learning. These learning procedures—modeling, role-playing, performance feedback, and generalization—have been used to teach a variety of behaviors, from academic competencies to sports to daily living skills. These procedures are applied in Skillstreaming to teach the child desirable prosocial behaviors.

Skillstreaming is not an affective education strategy that focuses primarily on discussion of feelings. Although discussion is a part, Skillstreaming engages children in active learning through role-playing and practice, actions that are more developmentally appropriate for children at this young age. Skillstreaming will not address all children's needs in every situation at all times. Instead, it is a well-validated teaching procedure that should be included with other techniques, such as behavioral support planning, conflict resolution, parent involvement and education, and cooperative learning. Nor is Skillstreaming a procedure for teaching compliance skills, the focus of some skills-training programs. Although it will teach students the skills needed to follow school rules and routines better, this program is mainly intended to teach children the skills needed to solve problems that occur in their daily lives, to be assertive in handling situations that cause them stress or unhappiness, and to increase the chance that they will have satisfying relationships with both peers and adults.

A SKILLS-DEFICIT MODEL

The Skillstreaming model makes the assumption that the learner is weak in or lacks a behavioral skill or skills. This model includes learners who have not yet acquired the prosocial behavior, those who may have knowledge of the behavior but are unable to perform it, and those who may perform the skill in some situations or under certain conditions but are unable to use it when its use is indicated (fluency/flexibility) or whose competing behaviors interfere with using the skill. The goal, in all such cases, becomes the active teaching of desirable skills.

We make this skills-deficit assumption for several reasons. First, the belief that most young children do not know how to act productively in given situations lessens the frustration many adults experience when these children seem continually to react in the same inappropriate way despite concentrated efforts to eliminate problem behaviors through the application of negative consequences. With other skills acquisition, such as academic or athletic skills, it is widely accepted that direct instruction is needed. As with any teaching endeavor and as the research on "brain-friendly" learning shows us, new learning is more likely to take place when it occurs in an encouraging, supportive, and nonthreatening environment. When children experience fear or feel that they are being threatened—for example, when teachers or other adults engage in verbal reprimands—the brain "downshifts" (Brendtro, Brokenleg, & Van Bockern, 1998; Goleman, 1995; Jensen, 2000). The more primitive parts of the brain, which deal with emotions, take control. Thus children react to the interaction in an emotional manner, often with a "flight or fight" response, and learning is improbable if not impossible. Some children may have knowledge of the skill but do not perform that set of behaviors on a consistent and relevant basis. Some teachers or researchers may argue that these children have performance or motivational deficits—not skills deficits. We are reminded of the words of a parent of a child with Attention Deficit/Hyperactivity Disorder who remarked, "The worst thing that happened to my child at school was that he had a good day!" After the child had succeeded, the expectation was that, if he could do it once, he could do it every day. Yet we know that for children with attention deficits, as well as for most children who experience behavioral difficulties, this is a faulty assumption. Providing direct instruction in prosocial skills will shift our energies into teaching and away from "expecting" and "consequating." In addition, children are far more likely to engage in learning a skill when they are taught in a deliberate and concentrated manner than when they wait for rewards that may not be forthcoming. Direct instruction will likely increase their motivation and performance consistency.

The skills-deficit assumption, then, allows adults to focus on proactive instruction instead of reacting to children's misbehavior as if it were done purposefully to create problems. In other words, it is recognized that it is more important to teach desirable skills than to punish children for inappropriate behaviors. This assumption, then, suggests that adults will be patient and encouraging while children learn these sometimes very difficult skills.

PLANNED, SYSTEMATIC INSTRUCTION

During the last decade, most educators have realized that children need to be taught desirable behaviors in the same planned and systematic way academic skills are taught. The reasons children do not learn acceptable social skills are many—including lack of knowledge, insufficient practice, insufficient reinforcement, emotional reactions that inhibit skill use (Cox & Gunn, 1980), and interfering or competing problem behaviors (Gresham, Sugai, & Horner, 2001). Incidental learning (such as discussing alternatives or telling children what to do) is insufficient for children to learn alternative behaviors and to perform these behaviors under stressful conditions, just as it is insufficient to tell children how to put letter sounds together and expect that they will be able to read. We further acknowledge that for the learning of many academic skills, the correct response is always correct (e.g., beginning letter sounds, math computation). The learning of social skills, however, is more complex, with a variety of potentially correct responses. Whatever the reason for skill lack or weakness, educators must establish and implement procedures to deliberately teach these skills, just as they would intervene to remediate academic or preacademic deficits.

SUMMARY

Teaching prosocial skills is a valuable intervention for any young child. The preschool and kindergarten child can be assisted in mastering daily school routines and can learn to follow through with adult expectations, solve interpersonal conflicts, and deal effectively with emotions. Just as we know we must teach young-sters to tie their shoes and understand that sounds are associated with the letters of the alphabet, so must we teach the behavioral skills that lead to happier school, home, and community experi-ences.

CHAPTER 2
Skillstreaming Program Directions

When confronted with children's aberrant behavior, educators often feel helpless and seek out referrals to other disciplines. Some educators do not realize that they have the abilities, skills, and strategies to greatly assist children with behavioral problems within the classroom and school-based setting. Understanding the development of Skillstreaming and how Skillstreaming fits into current educational practices should encourage educators to apply this strategy to help young children. This chapter describes the history and growth of Skillstreaming and offers some directions for current uses and future revision.

HISTORY AND DEVELOPMENT

The roots of psychological skills training, which began in the early 1970s, lie within both education and psychology. The psychoeducational approach viewed the child or client in educational terms, rather than as an individual in need of therapy, and assumed that the individual was deficient, or at best weak, in the skills necessary for effective and satisfying daily living. The task of the skills trainer, therapist, or teacher was the active and deliberate teaching of desirable behaviors. This view was in contrast to the assumptions of prior therapeutic approaches (psychodynamic, nondirective, or behavior modification), which held that the client possessed effective, satisfying, or healthy behaviors but that these behaviors were simply unexpressed.

Psychology's most direct contribution to psychological skills training came from social learning theory—in particular, the work of Albert Bandura. Bandura (1973) described the processes of modeling, behavioral rehearsal, and social reinforcement, and these processes directed the development of the Skillstreaming approach. Skillstreaming differed from the approaches of other behavior theorists, who emphasized operant procedures such as prompting and shaping of behaviors. Although a strictly behavioral approach was found to increase the frequency of a behavior, that behavior must already have been within the child's repertoire of behaviors. If the child did not have a grasp of the needed skill, operant procedures were insufficient to add that skill to the child's behavioral repertoire.

The deinstitutionalization movement of the 1970s, which resulted in the discharge of approximately 4 million persons from mental health and other institutions into local communities, further set the stage for acceptance of an alternative way of providing treatment. The realization was that the more traditional therapeutic interventions, which focused on looking inward to correct one's nonproductive actions (i.e., insight-oriented approaches), were ineffective for many individuals from lower socioeconomic environments, who constituted the majority of individuals discharged from institutions.

In addition to the growing importance of such structured learning methods in applied clinical work and as a preventive focus in community mental health, parallel developments in education clearly encouraged skills training. Specifically, a number of other approaches grew from the personal development context of certain educational movements—for example, progressive education (Dewey, 1938) and character education (Chapman, 1977). The goal of these approaches was to support the teaching of concepts and behaviors relevant to values, morality, and emotional functioning. We refer in particular to values clarification (Simon, Howe, & Kirschenbaum, 1972), moral education (Kohlberg, 1973), and affective education (Miller, 1976). These three approaches, as well as other personal growth programs, combined to provide a supportive climate and context for skills training. These programs share a concern for personal development, competence, and social effectiveness. Clearly, education had been broadened well beyond basic academic content to include areas traditionally the concern of mental health practitioners.

Since its initial development as an intervention prescriptively targeted to low-income adults deficient in social skills, Skillstreaming has increasingly been used with other populations. These populations have included young children (preschool and elementary age), elderly adults, child-abusing parents, industrial managers, police officers, and others. Over more than 25 years of program use, a considerable amount of evaluation research has been conducted and reported. The results of these several dozen studies support the efficacy of Skillstreaming, as well as suggest guidelines for altering and improving its procedures and materials. (An annotated bibliography of Skillstreaming research related to children and adolescents is presented as Appendix A in this book.)

CURRENT USES AND FUTURE DIRECTIONS

Skillstreaming is currently being used with children in many preschool and kindergarten classrooms, treatment programs, and day care settings across the country. Some school buildings and centers include instruction in Skillstreaming on a total-school basis, as part of a schoolwide—even districtwide—instructional and disciplinary program, with the goal of preventing school violence. It is our hope that Skillstreaming will continue to find success on a broader, more global basis throughout schools. The purpose of the following discussion is to describe the current uses of Skillstreaming and to present opportunities for its further use. It is our contention that Skillstreaming has broader application than the skills-training group or the classroom to change the way children interact with their world.

Violence Prevention

The issue of school violence is not reserved for middle schools and high schools. The greatest increase in school-related crime in the early 1990s occurred at the elementary level (Sautter, 1995). Fortunately, the majority of preschool and elementary school students do not experience violence, either as targets of violent acts or by observing violence in the school setting. However, many children do experience acts of aggression—as victims, observers, or aggressors.

Aggression and Bullying

One form of aggression that deserves closer scrutiny is bullying. Bullying is a common form of aggression encountered in preschool and elementary school classrooms (Manning, Heron, & Marshall, 1978; Smith & Levan, 1995). Bullying often begins in preschool (Beane, 1999) and presents significant behavioral issues not only for the young child who is the victim but for the bully and observers as well. The frequency of bullying in our schools is often underestimated (Atlas & Pepler, 1998). Bullying behavior has long been a concern in other countries, but only recently have schools in the United States come to understand its seriousness (Hoover & Oliver, 1996; Goldstein, 1999). As emphasized by Hoover and Oliver (1996), schools must be psychologically safe places, and bullying must be taken seriously.

It is important to distinguish between bullying and other types of aggression that may occur in the preschool and kindergarten setting. The most common form of bullying is teasing; however, occasional teasing does not constitute bullying. Neither is bullying considered rough play or accidentally hurtful events. Instead, in bullying there is a physical or psychological imbalance of power (Newman, Horne, & Bartolomucci, 2000), and it is often typified by rituals. The most accepted definition of bullying is presented by Olweus (1991), who states, "A person is being bullied or victimized when he or she is exposed, repeatedly and over time, to negative actions on the part of one or more persons" (p. 413). Goldstein (1999) adds to this definition by stating, "Bullying is harm-intending behavior of a verbal and/or physical character that is both unprovoked and repeated" (p. 69).

This type of aggression can be either direct or indirect (Olweus, 1993). Direct, or overt, bullying typically is observable verbal or physical aggression. Direct bullying includes hitting, pushing, kicking, and tripping, as well as the verbal behaviors of yelling, threatening, and cursing (Ahmad & Smith, 1994). Indirect bullying, on the other hand, is less easily observed but no less damaging to the victim. Indirect bullying includes behaviors such as spreading rumors, backbiting or scapegoating, and convincing others to ignore or isolate the victim.

Why should we be concerned with bullying at such a young age? Aren't such behaviors just a natural part of growing up? Walker, Colvin, and Ramsey (1995) address this issue:

Children who are at serious risk for developing antisocial behavior patterns . . . are often expected to "grow out of it." That is, maturity and the growth process are somehow expected to work a magical transformation in diverting the aggressive child from a path leading to antisocial behavior, conduct disorder, and delinquency. The evidence shows that young bullies often get worse and that instead of growing out of it, they actually grow into it. The best answer we seem to have is to attack this problem as early as possible. (p. 211)

Approximately one in seven schoolchildren is directly affected by bullying, as either bully or victim. This number does not include children who observe these acts of aggression and who may experience anxiety and fear that they may become the next victim. Indeed, as reported by Hoover and Oliver (1996), "75% to 90% of students looking back over their school careers report that they suffered harassment at the hands of fellow students" (p. 2). Not only does bullying create problems for the victims and observers, this pattern of aggression is believed to be a precursor to more severe and dangerous violence (Greenbaum, Turner, & Stephens, 1989; Hoover & Oliver, 1996; Olweus, 1991). Kauffman, Mostert, Trent, and Hallahan (1998) note that "engaging in aggressive antisocial acts is not good for children; it does not help them develop appropriate behavior, but increases the likelihood of further aggression, maladjustment, and academic and social failure" (p. 14). When ignored, bullying often escalates in intensity and continues in frequency (Goldstein, 1999).

Young children often engage in bullying or other aggressive acts to exert their power over others or to control a situation—for example, to get what they want, whether it is a toy, candy, a peer's lunch, or attention from peers. Bullying often is unreported because it typically occurs in places without sufficient adult supervision (e.g., playground, lunchroom, hallways, neighborhood park, to and from school). Many children do not report the aggression, perhaps for fear that they will receive even more aggression from the bully. Based on what adults often teach children, children are likely to question whether anything will be done about the provocation. After all, haven't adults reinforced the belief that children shouldn't tattle? Therefore, when a child does express his or her concerns and "tells on the bully," too often little or nothing is done to consequate (or provide alternatives to) the aggressor. Too many times it is the victim who is reprimanded by the adult, further rewarding the bully for the aggression.

Parents and teachers may also engage in bullying. Studies suggest that bullies often are exposed to physical punishment at home, are taught to "fight back" as a problem-solving strategy, and lack parental involvement and warmth (Banks, 1997). Additionally, approximately 1 in 10 teachers, by threatening and intimidating students, regularly engages in behaviors that constitute bullying (Goldstein, 1999). Adults in school environments may also contribute to bullying by what they fail to do, such as provide adequate supervision, respond when children make complaints, and enforce policies and procedures for handling such complaints.

How then do we, as educators, intervene to reduce bullying and other acts of aggression? Aggression is primarily a learned behavior. Natale (1994) states:

> Kids who commit violent acts often do so because they
> believe their choices are limited. . . . Psychologists say
> children with that view have learned aggression is a
> viable tool for resolving conflict—in fact, they've learned
> it's one of their only tools. (p. 38)

For some aggressive children, their acts are a "reasonable response," serving such functions as deterring becoming victims themselves, defying authority against perceived unfairness, and heightening their own sense of safety and security (Grant & Van Acker, 2000). As suggested by these authors, "Violence may be perceived as a legitimate or moral behavior by children placed in a situation in which they feel trapped or threatened either physically or psychologically. In such cases, violence is seen as a way to right a wrong" (p. 29). It may be surprising to some that one significant reason for aggression, bullying, and acts of violence is that children may have learned that this is their only way to respond. However, aggression is a remarkably stable behavior. Aggressive, antisocial behaviors, once learned and working, produce more of the same in the absence of prosocial alternative behaviors.

The goal of Skillstreaming is to teach prosocial alternatives. How can this strategy help children who are involved as victims, observers, or bullies? By experiencing direct teaching of behavioral skill steps, children who are victims or observers can learn assertiveness skills to deal effectively with being teased and with other peer provocation (Using Brave Talk, Skill 3; Dealing with Teasing, Skill 27), to tell an adult about a problem (Knowing When to Tell, Skill 35), to problem solve (Solving a Problem, Skill 30), and to say no (Saying No, Skill 38). Other skills from the Skillstreaming curriculum also may be effectively used in bullying contexts.

The bully also deserves our attention and instructional efforts. The bully, although often maintaining a level of social status with peers (Hoover & Oliver, 1996), often feels isolated from others. It is important to expand this child's repertoire of choices by teaching skills such as friendship making (Group III skills) as well as ways to deal with anger (Dealing with Feeling Mad, Skill 28) and other feelings (Group IV skills). In addition, because the bully seeks power or control, he or she can be given influence in a prosocial, positive way by helping to teach the skills to peers or younger children, or in other ways assuming a leadership role in Skillstreaming.

In addition to providing direct instruction in prosocial skills, dealing effectively with bullying requires the development of policies and procedures. When bullying occurs, a higher level of supervision is needed in those areas and activities, and adults must model positive ways of handling conflict. Yet we know that teachers and other adults cannot be available in all such situations on a consistent basis. Skillstreaming can therefore teach children the skills they need to cope effectively with bullying in their early childhood years and beyond.

Parent Involvement

From their early years, some children live with families and peers who repeatedly model, reward, and even overtly encourage hurtful actions toward others. In a real sense, aggression becomes for many children a behavior that "works"—both for them and for the significant people in their lives. As stated earlier, aggression is a difficult behavior to change. It is primarily a learned behavior, and many children have learned it well. John Reid, clinical psychologist and director of the Oregon Social Learning Center in Eugene, has analyzed numerous studies suggesting that the two strongest predictors of violence and delinquency are (a) ineffective, harsh, abusive emotional discipline and (b) lack of parental supervision (Bourland, 1995). Patterson, Reid, Jones, and Conger (1975) have discussed these actions by describing a cycle of aggression that begins, for some children, with coercive parenting. In this cycle, the parent frequently reacts to the child in a hostile, threatening, or irritated manner. The parent is inconsistent in his or her discipline, at times providing very strict supervision and at other times providing almost no supervision at all. Discipline is characterized by yelling and corporal punishment. At times the child will comply with the parent's coercion, thus providing a natural reward for the parent's disciplinary action. At other times, the child will act coercively in return—yelling, threatening, hitting, and so on. And on some occasions, the parent complies with the child's aggression, thus rewarding it and encouraging its continuation.

As children so parented grow older, they deal with peer confrontations in a similar manner. If they want a toy, they take it. If they don't like something another child has said, they hit or kick. Other children (or these children's parents) react by not including aggressive youngsters, thus limiting the positive models from whom these children can learn alternative behaviors and leading to social isolation. As these problematic children reach school age, they fulfill their need to have friends by seeking out peers who react similarly. An aggressive style of interaction may generalize, becoming a part of these children's behavioral repertoire with peers and teachers in the school setting. Thus the main characteristics of children who are the targets of coercive parenting are inadequate social skills and high levels of aggression, both in and out of school.

In school, agency, and other institutional settings, many chronically aggressive youths participate in interventions like Skillstreaming, designed to teach prosocial alternatives. They learn to maintain self-control or walk away from confrontations rather than incite, attack, or fight. They then use one of these prosocial alternatives in the presence of a family member or neighborhood peer, and, rather than reward the constructive attempt, the other party responds critically: "No son of mine is going to be a punk. You hit him before he hits you!" for example.

Program evaluations have suggested that children's prosocial responses are more likely to be rewarded, supported, and even reciprocated if significant others also participate in Skillstreaming training programs. Some of these joint efforts have involved teaching empathy skills to adolescents and their parents (Guzzetta, 1974) and teaching delinquent youths and their families alternatives to aggression (Goldstein, Glick, Irwin, Pask-McCartney, & Rubama, 1989). The success of these programs strongly suggests the effectiveness of instruction for both skill-deficient youths and the significant people in their lives. Chapter 10 describes additional considerations and gives suggestions for involving parents in the Skillstreaming process.

Learning Climate

An important component of violence prevention programs is a welcoming and positive learning climate. The climate or culture of a school reflects the prevailing set of values and beliefs held by school staff, parents, and students. These values and beliefs define acceptable behavior and determine the manner in which the preschool or kindergarten should function.

How does the culture of the learning environment relate to violence? As stated by Modro (1995):

> The most important factor that needs to be addressed even before policies that will support school safety is the atmosphere, or "feeling tone," in which education takes place. Does our educational system reflect a genuine belief in the essential dignity of each child? Do educators believe in the inherent value of the people they serve? The fear is that many mirror for our children what some of them already see reflected in society. (p. 11)

A cycle of conflict similar to the one described by Patterson et al. (1975) in the home environment can often be seen in school. The child who refuses to follow directions in school may be publicly and loudly reprimanded by the teacher. The one who verbally threatens to hit a peer may be threatened by the teacher with punishment. Such actions by adults may intensify the student's anger and problematic behavior (Gemelli, 1996). A power struggle may result in the child's exclusion from the learning environment, thus furthering the social isolation the child may already feel.

In their text on school reform, Golarz and Golarz (1995) urge schools to address the question "How can schools provide children with the tools to live personally satisfying and enriching lives?" (p. 11). Wilson and Daviss (1994) further suggest that schools include curricular approaches that teach children "to work together productively and manage controversy and disagreements in positive ways" (p. 186).

With the participation of a group of school personnel, schools must develop strategies to teach prosocial skills, increase student motivation, move toward problem solving rather than rote learning, enhance the relevancy of the curriculum, and make modifications related to students' interests and learning styles. Even though schools have the best of intentions, the typical authoritarian school structure may actually foster students' feelings of powerlessness. Lantieri (1995), in describing the Resolving Conflict Creatively Program, states that teachers must learn to deal with conflict in new ways and that "even more difficult, they must adopt a new style of classroom management, one that fundamentally involves a sharing of power with students so that they can learn how to deal with their own disputes" (p. 4).

Learning environments need to create opportunities for children to participate in rule setting and to accept responsibility, and children must be taught the skills necessary for prosocial participation in these activities. Creating a better balance of positive to negative consequences is also necessary to foster a positive school climate. Some children, in particular those who have well-established patterns of undesirable behavior, are most likely to receive an overabundance of negative consequences. For these individuals, positive feelings about school and learning itself are unlikely. Such children need more instruction, not less. Skillstreaming can provide this much-needed instruction and, if implemented widely, can help to shift the emphasis from punishment for negative behavior toward natural reward for positive behavior. In addition, positive, nonaggressive behaviors and problem solving must be modeled by school staff and reinforced when demonstrated by young students.

As discussed, many of the factors contributing to aggression in preschool and kindergarten settings lie outside the child and are within our control to change. Preventing and dealing effectively with the aggression of young children requires knowledge and understanding of the seriousness of such aggression. All preschool and kindergarten programs need policies and procedures to deal with aggression when it does occur, along with skills training to promote prosocial alternatives and positive relationships with both peers and adults, parent involvement and training, and group management strategies to foster a positive learning climate. At times, however, such schoolwide programs are insufficient to meet the needs of individual children. In such cases, comprehensive and individualized programs, such as Positive Behavioral Support Plans, are indicated.

POSITIVE BEHAVIORAL SUPPORT PLANNING

Interventions dealing with student behavior problems typically have focused on strategies to diminish or extinguish the behaviors of concern (e.g., time-out procedures, loss of privileges). This "curriculum of control" (Nichols, 1996) has been of concern to special educators, inasmuch as the approach is likely to be found in many general and special education classrooms. Although negative consequences may be a useful part of a comprehensive behavioral support plan, their use may further discourage children with behavior problems. Reinforcement strategies are used to increase positive behaviors; however, a given behavior must be displayed before it can be rewarded. Therefore, many children with infrequent appropriate behaviors rarely receive positive reinforcement; in most cases, they continue to receive an abundance of negative feedback.

Although typical behavior management programs are useful, necessary, and very often effective in reducing problem behaviors, emphasis on such programs alone may reinforce in students the idea that adults are the dispensers of rewards and punishments. Children may learn that whatever they might do, or however they might act, the positive or negative results of these actions will be determined by someone else in power—a teacher, parent, or other adult. Such a belief, referred to as an "external locus of control," can foster feelings of helplessness. The opposite is true when students learn, for example, to handle conflict in ways that yield approval from others. In this case, they learn a sense of responsibility and control (i.e., an "internal locus of control"). They more easily make the connection between their actions (e.g., use of a skill) and the forthcoming positive consequences.

Positive Behavioral Support Planning is a process for developing a comprehensive intervention plan to meet children's assessed behavioral skill needs. Such plans, based on an assessment of the purpose or function of undesirable behaviors, typically put in place a variety of supports. These include teaching children a replacement skill (an appropriate behavioral or social skill that will achieve the same goal as the misbehavior) and general social, academic, and coping skills. This approach to behavioral intervention planning is mandated by the 1990 reauthorization of the Individuals with Disabilities Education Act (IDEA) for special education students whose problematic behaviors are likely to result in disciplinary action. Although this approach is useful for special education students, it has also been found to be effective in facilitating change for children in general education classrooms.

Teaching prosocial skills provides children with opportunities to be successful in both hypothetical and real-life situations and lends a sense of balance to behavioral support programs. Although inappropriate behaviors will continue to need intervention, through Skillstreaming, children have the opportunity to build alternative, socially acceptable behaviors. Teachers and other adults will also find that prompting children to use a previously learned social skill when problematic situations arise in the classroom or in other settings will often stop children's inappropriate actions in midstream and channel their energies in a more prosocial direction. Like reminding students to think of a key word when being shown a letter of the alphabet, when given in a helpful and encouraging manner, such prompting fosters a positive learning climate and ultimately results in more efficient learning.

SUMMARY

The literature on violence prevention is encouraging in that it shows aggression and violence to be primarily learned behaviors. What better place to provide alternatives and help children learn that nonaggressive choices exist than in our schools? Although it may be discouraging to realize that poor parenting skills and supervision appear to play such an important role in the growth of violence, schools can intervene to address these concerns—for example, by increasing parent involvement. Furthermore, school personnel can address the areas that can be changed within the school, such as working to improve the school culture and moving toward a less authoritarian management style.

Schoolwide intervention programs to prevent violence (e.g., conflict management, social skills training, problem-solving training) have the potential to make a difference. One goal of such approaches is "to give everyone involved in the school the same skills, language and terminology for handling stress and conflict—to create an environment that is consistently nonviolent and nurturing" (Ascher, 1994, p. 4). When classwide and schoolwide programs do not result in the necessary behavioral change, individual interventions designed to provide children with additional support can be developed and implemented. The educational approach to prevention, in which emphasis is placed on teaching students the skills they need to deal with conflict and to get their needs met in prosocial ways, offers the best hope for the future.

CHAPTER 3

Skillstreaming Arrangements

This chapter describes the procedures necessary to plan and begin Skillstreaming at the preschool and kindergarten levels. Discussion concerns the specific arrangements to maximize the effectiveness of Skillstreaming instruction and the settings in which it occurs. In particular, we consider group leader selection and preparation; student selection and grouping; the role of support staff and parents in instruction; and specific instructional concerns such as skill selection, setting, materials, and instructional variations.

GROUP LEADER SELECTION AND PREPARATION

Since Skillstreaming began, hundreds of persons with a wide variety of backgrounds and positions have been effective group leaders. Teachers, counselors, and psychologists in the schools; youth care workers in treatment facilities; and social workers in mental health and other community agencies are primary examples. Regardless of the professional role of the leader, in any instructional group focusing on skill building, several competencies are necessary for effective instruction. These include (a) general teaching skills, (b) a knowledge and understanding of Skillstreaming procedures, (c) skills in managing behavior problems in positive and encouraging ways, and (d) a cultural understanding of the group participants.

General Teaching Skills

In the Skillstreaming group, as in any learning environment, effective teaching skills are necessary. The process involved in

Skillstreaming—modeling, role-playing, performance feedback, and generalization—is the same sequence used when teaching a child any other skill, such as self-help skills (e.g., tying shoelaces) or academic behaviors (e.g., beginning reading or math skills). The competent classroom teacher, therefore, already possesses the necessary background to carry out Skillstreaming.

As in teaching any other skill or subject content, the teaching agenda, as described in chapter 4, is delivered in a clear and organized manner. Transitions from one activity to another are smooth, the lesson moves at an energetic pace, children are actively engaged, and the relevance of skills to children's real-life needs is emphasized. The teacher listens to what the children are saying, gives feedback to let the children know their views have been heard, and adjusts instruction according to the needs of the learners. Furthermore, the effective teacher believes in what he or she is teaching and demonstrates enthusiasm, thus conveying an excitement in learning.

Another quality of effective teaching, also a component of group processing, is the ability to manage the diverse concerns or behavior problems that may arise throughout the teaching process. One child may have difficulty paying attention, another child may want to talk about an unrelated topic, and still another child may wander about the room, reluctant to participate at all. The skilled teacher is able to respond to such events in a firm, helpful, and unobtrusive manner and to maintain the flow of instruction. Strategies for preventing and reducing the frequency or intensity of problematic behaviors that are nonresponsive to the general instructional procedures are presented in chapter 9.

In addition, teaching will be more effective if it occurs in an encouraging, positive classroom environment. Skill learning will also be more likely to endure, and the skills more likely to be used in the child's real world, by applying the strategies included in chapter 8 and by involving significant others (e.g., parents) in the child's learning (chapter 10).

Knowledge of Skillstreaming

In addition to the general teaching skills just described, what specific knowledge is needed to make Skillstreaming instruction most effective? The following list describes the areas of preparation teachers or other leaders of Skillstreaming groups need, including skills and knowledge to implement the defined procedures.

1. Knowledge of Skillstreaming background, goals, and procedures

2. Ability to orient participating children, support staff members, and parents to Skillstreaming

3. Ability to assess student needs and select skills relevant to children's real-life needs, emphasizing assertiveness and problem-solving skills

4. Ability to plan and present live modeling displays, including presentation of a coping model and verbal mediation techniques

5. Ability to initiate and sustain role-playing

6. Ability to present material in a sequential, clear, and detailed manner

7. Accuracy and sensitivity in providing encouragement and corrective feedback

8. Willingness to accept children's use of the prosocial behaviors

9. Sensitivity to situations throughout the day in which skills could be used and prompting of appropriate skill use

Teachers and other group leaders may learn the background, goals, and procedures of Skillstreaming in a variety of ways, depending upon their own learning styles. Some may read and study this Skillstreaming program text, then be ready to begin. Most other potential teachers of Skillstreaming will find that attending a workshop or training session, viewing the demonstration of real-life groups in operation presented in *The Skillstreaming Video* (Goldstein & McGinnis, 1988), and/or listening to others who have implemented the techniques successfully augments what they have read.

A frequent question from workshop participants is "Can one teacher alone successfully lead a Skillstreaming group?" The best answer to this question is "It depends." Whether or not an individual teacher will be successful depends on his or her skill in group management as well as the skill deficiencies of the students. Though many Skillstreaming groups have been productively led by one teacher, we recommend that, whenever possible, two staff members work together, at least during the initial stages of instruction. To arrange and conduct a role play between two children while at the same time overseeing the attention of other, easily distractible group members can be daunting. A much better arrangement involves two teachers (or one teacher and another adult, such as a paraprofessional, volunteer, or school support staff member). Most often the classroom teacher functions as the main teacher, leading the modeling and role plays, while the second sits in the group, preferably next to the child who is most likely to have attention problems or act disruptively. Facets of Skillstreaming that take place outside the training setting—implementing generalization techniques, for example—are most effectively accomplished by the classroom teacher throughout the school day, and, for this reason, the teacher must take the leadership role within the training setting.

Managing the Group

A variety of activities included in Skillstreaming will keep the enthusiastic attention of most preschool and kindergarten children within the recommended time frame (20 minutes for preschoolers and 25 minutes for kindergartners). It is helpful, however, to offer the children a special sticker (to be put on their clothing or on a classroom chart) or another small reward on completion of each session for behaviors such as participating, listening, providing feedback, and following classroom rules. If classroom rules have not been previously identified, they should be decided upon prior to implementing Skillstreaming groups, discussed daily with the children to ensure understanding, and posted in the classroom. Rewarding such behaviors with small, material rewards, in addition to praising children's efforts, will help children feel positive about learning new prosocial behaviors.

Should behavioral concerns surface in the large group, a total-group management plan may be implemented. This type of plan might consist of dropping marbles in a jar when the group as a whole or specific youngsters show the desired behaviors, then providing a special activity for the entire group (e.g., extra recess) when the jar is full. Such plans may motivate the group to work cooperatively and may also increase the children's individual motivation. Youngsters who have disabilities relating specifically to behavior, as well as others who frequently exhibit behavior problems, may need an even more structured plan to reinforce desirable group behaviors.

Cultural Understanding

Which specific behaviors ideally define a given Skillstreaming skill? Which skills are optimal in any given setting? The answers will vary from culture to culture. Culture is defined by geography, ethnicity, nationality, social class, gender, sexual orientation, age, or some combination thereof. For Skillstreaming to be meaningful, it must be viewed and practiced within a multicultural context. To provide instruction with the necessary cultural sensitivity, Cartledge & Milburn (1996) state that the teacher needs to have an understanding of "the ways in which the learners have been socialized in other environments such as the family or the community, and the interference of this alternative socialization with the trainers' goals and the culture of the school and the mainstream society" (p. 1). Additionally, the teacher must be aware of cultural differences so he or she can determine which behaviors are in actuality social skills deficits and which behaviors are a part of the child's culture and should either be appreciated as they are displayed or be modified according to specific situations (Cartledge & Milburn, 1996). When the teacher and student are members of or are only minimally familiar with different cultural groups, definitions and prescriptions may conflict. Learning goals may not be met. For example, youngsters may engage in verbal bantering that appears to observers from a different cultural orientation to be aggressive. Yet these behaviors may be common and acceptable in their culture. In such an instance, the behaviors themselves do not need to be changed; instead, instructional emphasis may need to focus on when and where such verbal exchanges are appropriate within the school context.

In addition to addressing ethnic differences, Payne (1998) describes the culture of poverty. Referring to the hidden rules of generational poverty, Payne states that poverty is more about other resources (emotional, mental, spiritual, physical, support systems, knowledge of middle-class hidden rules, role models) than it is about money. For example, hidden rules of poverty suggest a high value on relationships and strong beliefs in fate or destiny. Skillstreaming leaders need to understand poverty as well as other cultures. Cartledge and Feng (1996) encourage teachers to "validate cultural background, making sure learners understand that certain situations will call for different responses, not that their ways of doing things are inferior" (p. 112).

Classrooms in this country are increasingly characterized by different languages, cultures, and learning styles. To reach all students, skilled administrators (and teachers) will to the degree possible employ materials that are consistent with a diversity of backgrounds and learning styles (i.e., "appropriate") and that have been selected in active and continuing consultation with persons representing the cultural groups concerned (i.e., "appreciative"). Appropriate and appreciative programming also applies to interventions designed to reduce student aggression. In discussing social skills interventions and what educators can do to interact with a culturally diverse student population, Cartledge and Johnson (1997) state:

> Social skill interventions are not to be viewed as a means for controlling students for the comfort of teachers or for homogenizing students so they conform to some middle-class prototype designated by the majority group in this society. Inherent in the concept of culturally-relevant social skill instruction is a reciprocal process where the educator: (a) learns to respect the learner's cultural background, (b) encourages the learner to appreciate the richness of this culture, (c) when needed, helps the learner to acquire additional or alternative behaviors as demanded by the social situation, and (d) similarly employs and practices the taught behaviors. (p. 404)

Skillstreaming will be most effective when it reflects awareness of issues associated with skill strengths and differences versus skill deficits, differential teaching strategies and instructional methods, student channels of accessibility and communication styles, stereotyping of and by culturally different student populations, and culturally associated characteristics of target students. In order to deliver the program in a manner appreciative of and responsive to cultural factors, teacher knowledge, skill, and sensitivity are required.

STUDENT SELECTION AND GROUPING

Student Selection

Student selection involves a twofold assessment task: First, if not all of the children in the class will be included, the task is to identify those who can benefit from direct instruction in skill building. The second part of the assessment task is to determine students' levels of proficiency in necessary skills. The selection process for young children may involve a number of assessment strategies, including sociometrics, behavior rating scales (teacher, parent, child), naturalistic observation, rubrics, and skill checklists. These last three strategies are the most user friendly and the least obtrusive and are the ones that lead most directly from assessment to instruction. It is important to remember, however, that assessment results are most useful when more than one type of evaluation procedure is used and when children's strengths and deficits are assessed in a variety of situations and settings and by a variety of individuals (e.g., peers, adults, parents).

In most Skillstreaming programs, assessment has typically involved each child's teacher and parent, as well as the child. It is common, however, for a discrepancy between adult and child ratings to occur. Whether such a discrepancy reflects overconfidence, denial, blaming others, lack of ability to assess one's own skills, or some other process in the child's or adult's perception, it is important to get the perspective of each child on his or her own skill strengths and weaknesses, either through verbal interaction or via a skills checklist. Teaching the skills the student believes necessary has proven to be a major motivational strategy.

Direct observation

Direct, or naturalistic, observation involves observing what the child does at particular times or in particular situations. Such observations, easily implemented by a classroom teacher, might involve taking frequency counts (e.g., how often a child deals with being teased or reacts to frustration in a particular manner), recording duration (e.g., how long it takes for a student to decide on something to do or the length of a crying episode), or making anecdotal records (e.g., what specific behaviors are of concern and their antecedents and consequences). Direct observation is especially valuable if the person or persons (teachers, youth care workers, etc.) who are planning to serve as group leaders are the same persons who are with the child all day and routinely see the child in interactions with others. In such circumstances, the behavioral observations can be frequent, take place in the child's natural environment, and reflect skill competence across diverse settings and situations. Direct observation is one method that is also advocated in assessing the goal or purpose of the child's behavior (i.e., conducting a functional behavioral assessment). Seeking to determine the student's motivation for engaging in a given maladaptive behavior will better help the adults who work with the child develop alternative, prosocial behavior plans, strategies, and skills to serve the same function for that child.

Skill checklists

Skill checklists are designed to assess various individuals' perceptions of a student's skill proficiency. Checklists for teachers and other school staff, parents, and students are included in Appendix B. The Teacher/Staff Skillstreaming Checklist is completed by a teacher or another person in the school environment who is familiar with the student's behaviors in a variety of situations. The rater is asked to gauge the frequency of the particular student's use of each of the 40 Skillstreaming skills. The checklist also provides an opportunity for the rater to identify situations in which skill use is particularly problematic, information that will be useful for later modeling scenarios.

The Parent Skillstreaming Checklist, also in Appendix B, seeks to assess the parent's perceptions of the child's skill needs in the home and neighborhood. Like the Teacher/Staff Skillstreaming Checklist, this rating scale allows the parent to respond to descriptions of the 40 prosocial skills in terms of the frequency of skill use. Even though information relative to the child's skill use outside of the school setting may be very useful, some discretion in requesting a parent to complete this checklist is necessary. The complete checklist may be given, or specific questions on the checklist may be selected to assess the child's strengths and weaknesses in skill areas that are of concern. Others may wish to use the checklist in an interview format with the parent. In whatever manner the Parent Skillstreaming Checklist is used, it may solicit valuable information regarding the child's skill competence and serve as a method to increase parent involvement.

When used with the Child Skillstreaming Response Record, the Child Skillstreaming Checklist (in Appendix B) is designed to assess children's own perceptions of the skills they feel they want or need to learn. Most appropriate for children ages 5 and older, the checklist is designed to be read to the individual child or to small groups of children in four separate evaluation sessions. This checklist helps children identify what types of behaviors they will be working on and will increase their motivation if they see the skills as ones that have relevance to their lives.

Rubrics

Rubrics are rules or guides "by which students' performance or a product is judged" (Schmoker, 1999, pp. 78–79). The use of rubrics as an evaluation tool related to academic skills, content, and behaviors has become accepted practice in education. Using rubrics related to the acquisition of social skills is particularly useful for the following reasons:

1. Due to the qualitative nature of social skills, rubrics portray a better composite of skill acquisition, performance, and fluency than do more traditional social skills assessment measures. Rubrics offer descriptions of quality that are not necessarily included in other performance evaluations (Schmoker, 1999).

2. Proficiency in using selected social skills does not necessarily equate with social competence. Rubrics allow for a more comprehensive picture of a child's social interaction.

3. By providing a clear target or objective, rubrics encourage the Skillstreaming leader to include the more subtle aspects of social performance in instruction, aspects beyond the rote learning of individual skills.

4. Rubrics convey a clear description of social expectations to teachers, parents, and students.

5. A sequence from a lower quality to a higher quality of performance can be assessed.

Rubrics describing levels of performance offer a fixed scale and identify specific characteristics that describe performance at each point on the scale (Marzano, Pickering, & McTighe, 1993) and provide a clear description of what is to be taught. Rubrics also "provide useful, quantitative data on clear, carefully selected qualitative criteria" (Schmoker, 1999, p. 78). A rubric for assessing the social performance of preschool and kindergarten children is presented in Appendix C.

Student Grouping

Once selected for participation, how are the children grouped? We have relied most heavily on two grouping criteria. The first criterion is shared skill deficiency. It is useful to group students who share similar skill deficiencies or patterns of deficits. By doing so, instruction will provide more intense skill instruction in the areas those children most need. The Skillstreaming Grouping Chart (see Appendix B) is designed to summarize scores on the 40 social skills for entire classes, units, or other groups of children; it can readily be used to identify shared skill deficiencies.

The second grouping criterion concerns the generalization-enhancing principle of identical elements. This principle, discussed in greater detail in chapter 8, holds that the greater the similarity between the teaching setting and the real-world, or application setting, the greater the likelihood that the child will actually perform the skill outside of the instructional setting. This principle is operationalized by teaching Skillstreaming to all children in a particular class, living unit, or neighborhood group. Including all children in the group or class in Skillstreaming may also help those who may develop behavior problems later on and who could benefit from skill instruction but are not at the present time identified by teachers or others as having skill needs.

ROLE OF OTHERS IN INSTRUCTION

The effort to teach prosocial behavior should not go forward in isolation; teachers and their students are a part of a school, a center, or another larger setting. We have suggested ways to select and prepare staff members who will serve as Skillstreaming group leaders. What about the rest of the staff? They also have a meaningful role to play in this effort, even if they will not be serving as group leaders.

School Staff

The goal of changing the behaviors of aggressive, withdrawn, or immature students often succeeds only at a certain time and in a certain place. That is, the program works, but only at or shortly after the time of instruction and only in the place of instruction. Thus a program may make a child behave in more desirable ways during and immediately following the weeks of teaching, in the classroom where it took place. But a few weeks later—or in the school hallways, outside on the playground, on a field trip, at home, or elsewhere outside the classroom—the child's behavior may be as problematic as ever. This temporary success followed by a relapse to the old, negative pattern of behavior is a failure of generalization. Generalization failures are much more the rule than the exception with many children. During Skillstreaming instruction, students receive a great deal of support, encouragement, and reward for their efforts. However, between group sessions or after instruction ends, many students receive little support or other positive response.

The common failure of generalization is not surprising. However, this outcome can be minimized. Newly learned and thus fragile skills need not fade away after a Skillstreaming unit has ended. If attempts to use such skills in the real world are met with success (i.e., support, enthusiasm, encouragement, reward), children will be much more likely to continue using the skills. Teachers, school staff, community members, parents, friends, counselors, peers, school administrators, and others who work directly with children are in an ideal position to promote continued skill use. All of these individuals can be powerful "transfer coaches," helping to make sure the Skillstreaming curriculum turns into a long-term or even permanent gain. Following are some specific ways these individuals can assist.

Learning the program

All school or agency staff should become highly familiar with their institution's Skillstreaming program—its goals, methods, group leadership, and, especially, the skills themselves. Memos, faculty meetings, attendance at Skillstreaming workshops, hall corridor "Skill of the Week" posters, and other means by which information is typically disseminated to staff should be regularly employed. In these ways, the transfer coach's prompting, encouraging, reassuring, and rewarding behaviors will more accurately target student skill needs.

Prompting

Under the pressure of real-life situations, both in and out of school, children may forget all or part of the skills they learned earlier. If their anxiety is not too great or their forgetting too complete, all they may need to perform a skill correctly is prompting. Prompting is reminding children what to do (the skill), how to do it (the steps), when to do it (now or at another "good time"), where to do it (and where not to), and/or why to use the skill (the positive outcomes expected). For example, the lunchroom supervisor may prompt a student to ignore teasing, in the school hallways the principal may suggest that a student deal with not being first in line, and in the library the librarian may prompt a student to ask a question or offer help to a classmate. The school playground offers many opportunities for children to practice friendship-making skills and alternatives to aggression; playground supervisors need to take an active role in prompting skill use in such environments.

Encouraging

Offering encouragement to children assumes they know a skill but are reluctant to use it. Encouragement may be necessary, therefore, when the problem is primarily a lack of motivation rather than a lack of knowledge or ability. Encouragement can often best be given by gently urging children to try using what they know, by showing enthusiasm for their skill use, and by communicating optimism about the likely positive outcome of skill use.

Reassuring

For particularly anxious students, skill generalization attempts will be more likely to occur if the threat of failure is reduced. Reassurance is an effective threat reduction technique. "You can do it" and "I'll be there to help if you need it" are examples of the kinds of reassuring statements the transfer coach can provide.

Rewarding

The most important contribution by far that the transfer coach can make for skill generalization is to provide (or help someone else provide) rewards for correct skill use. Rewards may take the form of approval, praise, or compliments, or they may consist of special privileges, points, tokens, recognition, or other reinforcers built into a classroom's or school's management system. For example, one school successfully enhanced skill generalization by having all staff in the school distribute "Gotcha Cards" whenever they observed a student using a prosocial skill. All such rewards will increase the likelihood of continued skill use in new settings and at later times.

The most powerful reward that can be offered, however, is the success of the skill itself. For example, if after a student practices Accepting Consequences (Skill 31) a real-life interaction goes very well, that reward (the successful interaction) will help the skill transfer and endure more than any external reward can. The same conclusion, that success increases generalization, applies to all of the Skillstreaming skills. It is important for all adults and peers to react with behaviors that signal awareness of effective skill use. If transfer and maintenance become schoolwide goals—supported by staff, administrators, students, and parents—and all make a concerted effort toward this end, fragile skills will become lasting skills, and Skillstreaming will have been successful.

Program Coordinator

Even if teachers, students, and support staff are prepared and motivated to begin a Skillstreaming program, the participation of one more professional helps ensure a successful outcome. Many effective programs involve the appointment of a program coordinator or master teacher. It is unfortunately common for Skillstreaming programs to begin with appropriate organization, good intentions, and adequate enthusiasm, only to wind up being discarded a few months later because of a lack of oversight. The barrage of other responsibilities often placed on teachers and other frontline staff makes intervention programs more likely to fail in the absence of such guidance.

The program coordinator should be well versed in both Skillstreaming and program management. Her or his Skillstreaming responsibilities may include providing staff development, observing sessions, monitoring schoolwide progress, setting up specific generalization-increasing efforts, motivating staff, facilitating the gathering and distribution of materials, and handling the many other details upon which program success depends.

Parents

Parents can and should be an integral part of the Skillstreaming program. Initially, informing parents of program goals will help them better understand and support these instructional efforts. Young children often select role plays and homework assignments that depict problems at home, and children are likely to report to parents the new ways they are learning to handle such problems. Because situations that occur at home are included in program instruction, parents need to understand the purpose of the program and the manner in which such situations are being discussed. Potential misunderstandings can be averted if parents are aware of the purpose of the program, its procedures, and ways they may be involved in an ongoing manner.

Approaching skill instruction as a cooperative effort between parents and teachers will likely enhance communication and improve the relationship between home and school. Additionally, when children see that the skills they have learned at school are accepted and rewarded at home, they are more likely to use the newly learned behaviors in a variety of situations and environments, thus enhancing the success of teaching efforts. Because of the importance of involving parents and facilitating their participation in the Skillstreaming program, chapter 10 is devoted to this effort.

SPECIFIC INSTRUCTIONAL CONCERNS

Program planners and the teachers or others who carry out Skillstreaming instruction will need to consider the following mechanics of implementation.

Prerequisite Skills

The behavioral skills outlined in chapter 6 are designed for children 3 to 6 years of age and for older children if their social and cognitive development warrants. Although most children in this age group will be successful in learning the skills when provided Skillstreaming instruction, the teacher will need to consider a few prerequisites. Specifically, children selected should be able to (a) attend to an ongoing activity for a short period of time (15 to 20 minutes); (b) follow simple directions; and (c) understand basic language concepts such as *same, different, or,* and *not* (Spivack & Shure, 1974). Deficiencies in these competencies will need to be remediated by maturation or direct teacher efforts prior to these children's involvement in Skillstreaming instruction. However, young children who possess some of the prerequisites but who, for example, have difficulty attending for this time period in a group setting may benefit from skills instruction conducted on an individual basis. Likewise, children with deficits in language or communication skills may be included in the group instruction, but with special attention and instruction being given in areas such as understanding concepts and sequencing.

Skill Selection and Negotiation

We recommend that the group leader initiate instruction with the Beginning Social Skills (Group I). Several of the skills included in this group serve as behavioral steps for later skills or address important facets of skill performance, such as the way in which a skill is performed. Other skills in this group are frequently needed and will likely bring a positive outcome, thus validating the success of skills teaching for children and teachers alike.

Once the children have learned the Group I skills, other skills should be selected on the basis of the needs and problems the children experience. Although some will be eager to discuss areas of skill need for themselves or their peers (e.g., "Sam says I'm a baby, and I hit him"), it is often up to the teacher to plan group discussions that will facilitate the sharing of skill need. In addition, the children's responses on the Child Skillstreaming Checklist (in Appendix B) will provide information about the skills children feel they need and want to learn. Because the needs of the group may vary, one or more skills may be selected from each of the remaining five skill groups, with the sequence of instruction depending on the most critical needs of the majority of the children in the class or group. Allowing the children to identify their own areas of skill need and to use skills in ways that benefit them will help promote effective and enduring learning and will increase their desire to learn other skills.

Skills that are important to others in the child's environment, such as parents and other teachers, are considered next. Selection of skills valued in the home and neighborhood can be made easier by considering parents' responses on the Parent Skillstreaming Checklist (in Appendix B). Considering parent input in the selection decision may also help identify skills that, although beneficial in the school setting, may actually be contradictory to the expectations of the home and neighborhood. The teaching challenge then, in addition to teaching the skill itself, becomes to emphasize skill flexibility, or adjusting skill use to different people and different situations. Parent input will guide the teacher in emphasizing the specific settings in which a given skill will most likely be useful.

The teacher can select additional skills for instruction by observing difficulties the children are experiencing in following school routines, interacting with their peers, and dealing with situations involving stress or conflict. The Teacher/Staff Skillstreaming Checklist (in Appendix B) can be useful in identifying these problematic skill areas. Selecting skills needed in day-to-day school-related problem situations allows the teacher to coach or prompt the child through the skill at the very time skill use is indicated. This powerful strategy, termed *instructed generalization* or *capturing teachable moments,* greatly enhances skill learning and performance.

Teaching the prosocial skills valued by the children's parents and teachers (and, in some cases, by peers) increases the likelihood that natural rewards will be forthcoming in the real-world environment. Such rewards are likely to help children maintain their use of the skills once direct teaching is withdrawn.

Introduction of New Skills

To reduce the possible interference of new learning with previously learned material, the teacher should introduce a second skill only when the child can recall the steps of the first skill, has had an opportunity to role-play it, and has shown some initial generalization of learning outside the teaching setting. Therefore, it may be necessary to spend four or five sessions on one skill. In the case of more complicated skills, 2 or 3 weeks, or even longer, may be needed before proceeding to another skill. Periodic review of previously learned skills reinforces these skills and encourages their use in new situations, provides systematic fading of the teaching to enhance generalization (Buckley & Walker, 1978), and prevents boredom that may occur with concentration on only one skill for the time required for sufficient learning.

Instructional Setting

Ideally, the instructional setting for Skillstreaming will be the classroom, day care room, or other location where the child spends the majority of instructional and play time. Research provides two very important reasons in support of this recommendation. First, because the child's peers in this setting will also have received instruction, the child will be more likely to receive encouragement and assistance in actually using the skills. Second, because generalization from the teaching setting to the application setting does not occur automatically, teaching the skills in the environment in which the child will most often need the skills (i.e., the natural environment) promotes learning and skill maintenance. Alternative and typically less structured school areas—such as hallways, the playground, the school cafeteria, and the school bus—are good places to carry out instructional and practice sessions. When a given skill applies in an easily accessible school environment, modeling and role-playing should occur in that setting.

Occasionally, it may be necessary to provide skills instruction in another, more artificial environment, such as a counselor's office or a special education resource room. Although this type of instructional setting is less likely to promote long-term learning, teaching can and should be done if the child needs additional coaching to learn the skill. However, such settings are not recommended either for ongoing instruction or as the only setting for skills teaching.

A special space should be provided in the classroom for the initial instruction of each skill. This most often is an area of the classroom where the children can sit cross-legged on the floor in a semicircle, a configuration that allows all children to view the modeling displays and role plays. As with other types of group instruction, accommodations may need to be made to minimize the problematic behavior that may occur at this age level. These accommodations include having children sit in a clearly defined space (using tape on the floor or individual carpet samples), sit at a distance from a "best friend," and the like. Once the children can perform the skill in this somewhat artificial instructional setting, skills instruction can and should occur in other natural classroom settings (e.g., at tables or desks, play areas, or learning centers).

Time Factors

Frequency and length of sessions

At the preschool and kindergarten levels, skills training sessions should be held on a daily basis whenever possible. Approximately 20 minutes for preschoolers and 25 minutes for kindergarten children should be planned for each session, with the time of the sessions adjusted on the basis of the children's attention span, interest, and maturity. Many teachers have found it most beneficial to conduct a 15-minute session early in the day (e.g., immediately following the classroom opening activities) and another 10-minute session later on (e.g., following recess or lunch). Holding the Skillstreaming session early will give the children more opportunity to practice the newly learned behaviors throughout the remainder of the day. Additional time can be planned for supplemental activities related to skill performance, such as those suggested in chapter 6. Continued skill use will also be facilitated if an additional 5 minutes at the end of the day is allotted for teacher and students to chart the skills they have practiced throughout the day. This and other generalization-enhancing procedures are discussed in chapter 8.

Throughout the school day, in both structured and unstructured settings, the teacher may prompt, encourage, reassure, and reward children for using the behavioral skills. When a situation suggesting instruction in Skillstreaming arises, the teacher may choose to provide additional group or individual sessions. From this viewpoint, Skillstreaming is an ongoing effort, with initial instruction occurring at the time set for the group, and additional learning and generalization-enhancing procedures taking place throughout the school day.

Program duration

When Skillstreaming groups first began more than two decades ago, many practitioners implemented skills instruction for a few weeks, covering skills that appeared critical in the child's social development. More recently, it has been accepted that such instruction needs to be an ongoing part of the curriculum for young children in both general and special education programs. The 40 social skills included in chapter 6 may be taught repeatedly throughout successive school months or years, as the child's proficiency, flexibility, and use of the behaviors become more refined. Teachers or other group leaders may then progress to more advanced skills, such as those included in *Skillstreaming the Elementary School Child* (McGinnis & Goldstein, 1997).

Materials

Skillstreaming is not an expensive program to implement. A chalkboard or easel pad, Skill Cards listing the skill steps, and teacher-made skill-step posters to hang in the classroom and school are the core materials. Skill Cards may be of the preprinted variety available with the program (see the example in Figure 1); group leaders may also make these cards themselves.

A Program Forms book augments the basic Skillstreaming procedures and enhances their effectiveness. In a reproducible 8 ½ by 11–inch format, this book provides essential program forms, checklists, and awards to enhance generalization. Other materials to enhance the effectiveness of Skillstreaming instruction already exist in most classrooms. For example, if a game or particular toy is an important part of the role play, the actual object should be used

Figure 1 Skill Card

SKILL 26

Showing Affection

1. Decide if you
   have nice feelings.

2. Choose.

   a. Say it.

   b. Hug.

   c. Do something.

3. When?

4. Do it.

Skillstreaming in Early Childhood:
New Strategies and Perspectives for Teaching Prosocial Skills
© 2003 by Ellen McGinnis and Arnold P. Goldstein.
Champaign, IL: Research Press (800) 519–2707.

whenever possible. The use of such real-life materials is based on the important principle of identical elements, discussed in chapter 8. Briefly, this rule states that the greater the similarities between the teaching and application settings, the greater the likelihood that children will transfer skills from one setting to the other. For this reason, items the children normally have access to should be used in both modeling displays and role plays.

Instructional Variations

Historically, applications of Skillstreaming have been directed toward children selected from a larger classroom group. There are advantages to doing so, as well as other gains to be achieved from providing instruction to the whole class. Therefore, instruction may be carried out in large or small groups and occasionally, in special circumstances, with an individual child.

Large-group instruction

For two main reasons, it is best that all of the children in a given preschool or kindergarten class be involved in Skillstreaming instruction. First, teaching the whole group may prevent children from developing maladaptive patterns of behavior that may over time become more well established and thus more difficult to change. There is value in providing all children with skill strategies and prosocial behaviors on a preventive basis to enable them to handle future skill-relevant difficulties. Second, providing instruction to the entire class involves the use of socially competent peers as models for those children with skill deficits or weaknesses. If the situation is handled with sensitivity, including skilled peers gives the skill-deficient child a unique advantage. Because the effectiveness of modeling is enhanced when the model is similar to the observer in age and other characteristics, children who are adept in a skill may be more effective models than the classroom teacher. In addition, children who are more competent in skill performance can function effectively as coactors in the role plays.

General instruction, modeling displays, and the first several role plays can be successfully carried out in a group of 20 or more children. Subsequent role plays, sufficient to allow all children the opportunity to try out the skill under direct teacher guidance, are often carried out in two or more smaller groups, with an adult leader assigned to each group. With fewer children in a role-play group, more opportunity exists for each child to assume the role of the main actor and to receive constructive suggestions, encouragement, and reinforcement. The more practice a child has with a particular skill, the more likely he or she will be to apply that skill over time and in other environments. Thus the whole group meets first to generate skill-relevant situa-

tions, present the skill, discuss the skill, and conduct the modeling and one or two role plays. It is important not to stop the
instruction of the given skill at this point, however. Skillstreaming
is an experiential activity, and, as such, the role-playing is vital
for learning. Role plays, feedback, and homework must therefore
be done in smaller groups.

When working with large groups of children, teachers have
elicited assistance from other adults in the school (e.g., volunteers, school administrators, older children who act as peer
helpers, even custodians). Some preschool, day care, or special
education teachers may likely work with co-teachers or para-
professionals, but kindergarten teachers may not have such
help and may be faced with instructing the large group in all
aspects of Skillstreaming. In this circumstance, it is particularly
important that the teacher gain the attention and involvement
of as many children as possible. Teachers can encourage
involvement by assigning group-helper roles, such as pointing
out the skill steps on a teacher-made chart as they are being
role-played; encouraging children who are not active participants in the role play to watch for the enactment of specific skill
steps; and walking around these observers as much as possible
while still maintaining verbal involvement in the role play.
Others have found success by using several older students as
coactors in role plays or by asking an older peer helper to watch
for and provide feedback on particular skill steps. Still others
choose to teach Skillstreaming within the classroom, in a fash-
ion similar to traditional reading groups. In this variation, the
teacher introduces the skill and presents the modeling display
and one or two role plays to the whole group but conducts subsequent role plays, feedback sessions, and assignment of homework in small groups. Thus the teacher is able to spend time
with students who need extra practice in role-playing to learn
the skill.

Small-group instruction

Under certain circumstances, preschool and kindergarten children may be assigned to smaller groups according to common skill
needs. This will likely mean that participating children will not be

from the same classroom. Because role-playing is more effective when the teaching setting closely resembles the real-life environment, it is useful to include children whose social environments (e.g., peer groups) are similar. Selecting participants from a common peer group will not only make the role play more realistic, but will also increase the likelihood that the children will attempt the skill with peers in the classroom or neighborhood.

The ideal small group consists of eight or fewer students, depending upon student needs. If students exhibit particularly problematic behaviors, a more appropriate group size may be three or four students. If a smaller number is necessary due to members' aggression or out-of-control behavior, additional students may be added (perhaps at the rate of one new member per week) once the smaller group is operating successfully.

Small-group instruction is often carried out by a school counselor or other school support person. This type of setting and instruction is most beneficial if it provides added opportunities for skill learning and practice to those children who are in critical need of mastering the skills. Following this type of small-group instruction, it is most helpful if the children participate in whole-class instruction as well.

Individual instruction

Although Skillstreaming is primarily designed to be carried out in a group setting, in special cases modifications can be made to include one-to-one instruction. The child who needs additional help in learning a specific skill, who withdraws from group involvement, or who lacks the prerequisite skills for the group setting benefits from this type of instruction. For example, the child who bullies others can assume a leadership role in subsequent groups by first learning the skill via coaching and assisting the teacher in the modeling displays. When carried out individually, the Skillstreaming procedures remain the same, but the adult—or the child's peer if this is feasible—serves as the coactor in each role play and provides the feedback except for that elicited from the target child. Although individual instruction is a useful way of providing skills instruction to some children, the main objective should be to include all youngsters in a Skillstreaming group as soon as possible.

SUMMARY

This chapter has focused on the steps necessary to plan and organize effective Skillstreaming groups for preschool and kindergarten children. Selection and preparation of group leaders, student assessment and grouping, and the role of others—school staff, program coordinator, and parents—in Skillstreaming instruction have been described. Additional discussion has addressed specific instructional concerns: prerequisite skills, skill selection and negotiation, and introduction of new skills. Instructional setting, time factors, materials, and instructional variations have also been examined. Addressing these components in a comprehensive manner before implementing the Skillstreaming group will foster a reinforcing environment for skill learning for both participants and leaders.

CHAPTER 4

Skillstreaming Teaching Procedures

Carrying out the core Skillstreaming teaching procedures—modeling, role-playing, performance feedback, and generalization—involves leading the group through nine steps:

- Step 1: Define the skill
- Step 2: Model the skill
- Step 3: Establish student skill need
- Step 4: Select the first role player
- Step 5: Set up the role play
- Step 6: Conduct the role play
- Step 7: Provide performance feedback
- Step 8: Assign skill homework
- Step 9: Select the next role player

This chapter describes these steps and illustrates the Skillstreaming procedure in operation. Table 1 provides a more detailed summary of the steps for ongoing reference.

STEP 1: DEFINE THE SKILL

Most young children are likely to be more motivated to learn the behaviors presented in Skillstreaming instruction when they feel they need to learn a particular behavioral skill. For example, if a preschooler often feels that he is the brunt of teasing from peers, the child will be more highly motivated to learn Dealing with

Table 1 Outline of Skillstreaming Procedures

Step 1: Define the skill

1. Choose skills relevant to the needs of the children as they perceive them.

2. Discuss each skill step and any other relevant information pertaining to each step.

3. Use Skill Cards and/or a chalkboard or easel pad on which the skill and steps are written so all group members can easily see the steps and illustrations.

Step 2: Model the skill

1. Use at least two examples for each skill demonstration.

2. Select situations relevant to the children's real-life circumstances.

3. Use modeling displays that demonstrate all the behavioral steps of the skill in the correct sequence.

4. Use modeling displays that depict only one skill at a time. (All extraneous content should be eliminated.)

5. Show the use of a coping model.

6. Have the model "think aloud" steps that ordinarily would be thought silently.

7. Depict only positive outcomes.

8. Reinforce the model who has used the skill correctly by using praise or self-reward.

Step 3: Establish student skill need

1. Elicit from the children specific situations in which the skill could be used or is needed.

2. List the names of the group members and record the theme of the role plays.

Step 4: Select the first role player

1. Select as the main actor a child who describes a situation in his or her own life in which skill use is needed or will be helpful.

2. Provide encouragement and reinforcement for the child's willingness to participate as the main actor.

Step 5: Set up the role play

1. Have the main actor choose a coactor who reminds him or her most of the other person involved in the problem.

2. Present relevant information surrounding the real event (i.e., describe the physical setting and events preceding the problem).

3. Use props when appropriate.

4. Review skill steps and direct the main actor to look at the Skill Card or the skill steps on the chalkboard or easel pad.

5. Assign the other group participants to watch for specific skill steps.

Step 6: Conduct the role play

1. Instruct the main actor to "think out loud."

2. As needed, assist the main actor (e.g., point to each behavioral step as the role play is carried out; have the co-leader, if available, sit among the group members, directing their attention to the role play).

Step 7: Provide performance feedback

1. Seek feedback from the coactor, observers, leader(s), and main actor, in turn.

2. Provide reinforcement for successful role plays at the earliest appropriate opportunity.

3. Provide reinforcement to the coactor for being helpful and cooperative.

Table 1 (continued)

4. Praise particular aspects of performance (e.g., "You used a brave voice to say that").

5. Provide reinforcement in an amount consistent with the quality of the role play.

Step 8: Assign skill homework

1. Assign homework to the main actor if he or she has successfully role-played the skill.

2. Discuss with the main actor when, where, and with whom he or she will use the skill in real life.

Step 9: Select the next role player

Ask, "Who would like to go next?"

Teasing (Skill 27) than another skill not as immediately relevant. Information regarding relevant skills can be obtained by referring to the children's responses on the Child Skillstreaming Checklist (Appendix B), as well as by discussing with the group the day-to-day problems they encounter.

In a brief discussion activity, the teacher or other group leader presents the skill. The goal is for students to understand the skill in a general way. The presentation and discussion should be relatively brief because the attention span of this age group is short. The following types of questions will help stimulate appropriate discussion: "Who finds it hard to wait for a turn while playing a game?" "Why is this important to learn?" (Waiting Your Turn, Skill 16); "What does sharing mean?" "Is it hard for you to share a toy with someone else?" (Sharing, Skill 17); "Who can tell me what a mistake is?" "Who feels really mad after making a mistake?" (Dealing with Mistakes, Skill 33). This goal is typically achieved in only a few minutes of discussion when children are prompted with such questions.

The specific behavioral steps to achieve the skill are next presented and discussed briefly. The teacher should ensure that the participants understand the vocabulary included in the skill and have a general understanding of what they will be learning.

Children should receive a Skill Card (see Figure 1, on page 44), and/or the skill and corresponding steps should be written on a chalkboard or easel pad and displayed for the group.

It is important for the teacher to avoid giving a lecture when defining the skill. Although part of a teacher's job is to talk and explain, Skillstreaming must be carried out as an experiential activity, and defining the skill must be carried out with dispatch.

STEP 2: MODEL THE SKILL

Modeling is defined as learning by imitation. A great deal of research has consistently shown imitation to be effective and reliable for learning new behaviors and for strengthening or weakening previously learned behaviors. Three types of learning by modeling have been identified. *Observational learning* refers to the learning of behaviors a person has never performed before. Children are great imitators. Even very young children learn new behaviors by observing others (mostly peers), whether these are styles of dressing, ways of talking, play activities (e.g., house, school), or other positive or negative behaviors.

Inhibitory and *disinhibitory effects* involve the strengthening or weakening of behaviors previously performed only rarely by the person because of a history of punishment or other negative reactions. Modeling offered by peers is, again, a major source of inhibitory and disinhibitory effects, and it frequently results in children's succumbing to peer pressure. Children who know how to be altruistic and caring and the like may inhibit such behaviors in the presence of models who are behaving more egocentrically and being rewarded for their egocentric behavior. Aggressive models may have a disinhibitory effect: If a child sees another go unpunished for aggression, the observing youngster may engage in aggressive behavior as well.

Behavioral facilitation refers to the performance of previously learned behaviors that are neither new nor a source of potential negative reactions from others. One person buys something he or she seems to enjoy, so a friend buys one, too. A child deals with a confrontational peer in an effective manner, then a classmate approaches a similar problem the same way. These are examples of behavioral facilitation effects.

Research has demonstrated that a wide array of behaviors can be learned, strengthened, weakened, or facilitated through modeling. These include acting aggressively, helping others, behaving independently, interacting socially, displaying dependency, exhibiting certain speech patterns, behaving empathically, and more. It is clear from such research that modeling is an effective way to teach new behaviors.

Yet it is also true that most people observe dozens and perhaps hundreds of behaviors that they do not then engage in themselves. Television, radio, magazines, and newspapers expose people to very polished, professional modeling displays of someone's buying one product or another, but observers do not later buy the product. People observe expensively produced instructional videos, but they may not learn the skills depicted. Children may see many behaviors enacted by peers in a given school day but copy only a few or none.

Modeling Enhancers

Research on modeling has successfully identified what we call *modeling enhancers,* or conditions that increase the effectiveness of modeling. These modeling enhancers are characteristics of the model, the modeling display, or the observer (the student). These variables affect learning, as does use of a coping model.

Model characteristics. More effective modeling will occur when the model (the person to be imitated) (a) seems to be highly skilled or expert; (b) is of high status; (c) controls rewards desired by the observer; (d) is of the same sex, approximate age, and social status as the observer; (e) is friendly and helpful; and, of particular importance, (f) is rewarded for the behavior. That is, we are all more likely to imitate expert or powerful yet pleasant people who receive rewards for what they are doing, especially when the particular rewards involved are things we, too, desire.

Modeling display characteristics. More effective modeling will occur when the modeling display shows the behaviors to be imitated (a) in a clear and detailed manner; (b) in the order from least to most difficult behaviors; (c) with enough repetition to make overlearning likely; (d) with as little irrelevant detail as possible;

and (e) performed by several different models rather than a single one.

Observer (student) characteristics. More effective modeling will occur when the person observing the model is (a) told to imitate the model; (b) similar to the model in background or attitude toward the skill; (c) friendly toward or likes the model; and, most important, (d) rewarded for performing the modeled behaviors.

Coping model. Modeling is more effective when a coping model, or a model who has some difficulty achieving the goal of competent skill performance, is presented (Bandura, 1977). When demonstrating Dealing with Feeling Mad (Skill 28) or Saying No (Skill 38), it is important to show some emotion and to struggle a little with modeling. This struggle must be demonstrated in a low-key manner, and in an acceptable way, so it does not detract from the modeling display. However, if young children perceive that the skill is "easy" and can be performed without any feeling, they may be less likely to try the skill when caught up in the emotion of a real-life event. Depicting coping models will further enhance children's ability to identify with the model and will likely give them more courage to try the skill themselves.

Stages of Modeling

The effects of these modeling enhancers, as well as of modeling itself, can be better understood by considering the three stages of learning through modeling.

Attention. Children cannot learn from watching a model unless they pay attention to the modeling display and, in particular, to the specific behaviors being modeled. Students are better able to attend to the modeling if the display eliminates irrelevant detail, minimizes the complexity of the modeled material, makes the display vivid, and implements the modeling enhancers previously described.

Retention. In order to later reproduce the behaviors observed, the child must remember or retain them. Because the behaviors of the modeling display itself are no longer present, retention must occur by memory. Memory is aided if the behaviors displayed are classified by the observer. Another name for such classification is *covert rehearsal* (i.e., reviewing in one's mind the performance of the behaviors modeled). Research has shown, however, that an even more important aid to retention is *overt rehearsal* (i.e., behavioral rehearsal). Such practice of the specific behavioral steps in a skill is critical for learning and, indeed, is the second major procedure of Skillstreaming. This is role-playing, a procedure to be examined in more depth later in this chapter. It should be noted at this point, however, that the likelihood of retention by either covert or overt rehearsal is greatly aided by rewards provided to both the model and the observer.

Reproduction. Researchers in the area of learning have distinguished between learning (acquiring or gaining knowledge) and performance. If a person has paid attention to the modeling display and has remembered the behaviors shown, it may be said that the person has learned. However, the main interest is not so much that the person *can* produce the behaviors observed, but whether he or she *does* produce them. As with retention, the likelihood that a person will actually perform a learned behavior depends greatly on the expectation of a reward for doing so.

Modeling Guidelines

In planning live modeling displays, teachers should use at least two examples for each skill demonstration. If a skill is used in more than one group session, it is wise to develop two new modeling displays. The display should show situations relevant to children's real-life circumstances, and, as noted previously, the model (i.e., the person enacting the behavioral steps of the skill) should be portrayed as a child reasonably similar in age, socioeconomic background, verbal ability, and other characteristics salient to the children in the Skillstreaming group. Modeling displays should demonstrate all the behavioral steps of the skill in the correct sequence, use a coping model, and show positive outcomes. Finally, modeling displays should depict only one skill at a time, with no extraneous content, and the model using the skill well should always be reinforced.

In order to encourage young children to attend to the skill portrayals, Skill Cards like the one shown in Figure 1, which include the name of the skill being taught and its behavioral steps and corresponding illustrations, are distributed prior to the modeling displays. Students are asked to watch and listen closely as the modeling unfolds. Particular care should be given to helping children identify the behavioral steps as they are being modeled. Teachers and other group leaders can do this by pointing to the steps, which have been written on a chalkboard or easel pad, or by having the model state aloud the behavioral steps in the course of the modeling. Students should be reminded that models will often "think aloud" words that would normally be thoughts to oneself in order to depict the behavioral steps.

Verbal Mediation or "Thinking Aloud"

Thinking aloud what would normally be said to oneself silently, or *verbal mediation,* is a valuable and necessary part of both modeling and role-playing. Saying the steps aloud as the models or role players are enacting the behaviors demonstrates the cognitive processes underlying skill performance, helps curb impulsivity, and facilitates both initial learning and generalization of the skill (Camp & Bash, 1981, 1985). For example, in Joining In (Skill 15), the model might say, "I want to ask if I can play, but I'm afraid they might say no. But I'm going to try. OK, the first step is to watch." Likewise, in Knowing When to Tell (Skill 35), the model would recite the skill steps in the context of the situation—for example, "Those kids are teasing Jessie. They shouldn't do that. It's a problem, but should I tell? What's the first step?" This type of accompanying narration increases the effectiveness of the modeling display (Bandura, 1977), draws the attention of the observers to the specific skill steps, and may facilitate generalization of the skill (Stokes & Baer, 1977). Verbal mediation also helps to demonstrate a coping model. For example, in Waiting Your Turn (Skill 16), the model might say aloud, "It's hard to wait, but I can do it." Many young children will need to be taught the process of thinking aloud by having them practice while they are engaged in other types of activities (e.g., "Which picture goes with the dog? Look at all of them. Is it the chair? No. Keep looking").

STEP 3: ESTABLISH STUDENT SKILL NEED

Behavioral rehearsal is the purpose of the role play. Before group members begin role-playing, it is important to identify each child's current and future need for the skill. Reenactment of a past problem or circumstances is less relevant than current and future need, unless the student predicts that such circumstances are likely to reoccur in the future. Current skill needs will probably have been established earlier as part of the skill selection process (e.g., through use of the skill checklists). Nonetheless, a discussion within the class or group is needed to establish relevant and realistic role plays. Each student is in turn asked to describe briefly where, when, and with whom he or she would find it helpful to use the skill just modeled. (*Note:* Instruction with a large group requires that those children who will be role-playing give such information during each session. More than one or two sessions will be needed for all students to offer this information and be the main actor in a role play of the target skill.)

To make effective use of this information, it is often valuable to list the names of the group members on the chalkboard or easel pad at the front of the room and to record next to each name the general theme of the role play. With children at this young age, especially when Skillstreaming is new, the teacher or other group leader may need to ask leading questions to prompt the generation of skill situations. Such questions could include "I notice that many kids have difficulty ignoring when at the listening center. How many of you think you need to practice this skill at the listening center?"

STEP 4: SELECT THE FIRST ROLE PLAYER

All members of the Skillstreaming group will be expected to role-play each skill taught; therefore, in most cases it is not of great concern who does so first. Typically, teachers may ask for volunteers to begin the series of role plays. If for any reason there are children who appear to be reluctant to role-play a particular skill on a particular day, it is not necessary to ask them to be one of the first. Observing others can be reassuring and may help them ease their way into the activity.

In general, young children should be encouraged, reassured, and reminded to use the skill to meet their own needs, rather than penalized, threatened, or otherwise coerced into participation. When confronted with a reluctant participant, many teachers of young children have found that coaching the child through the role play on a one-to-one basis outside of the group or allowing the student initially to participate in another manner (e.g., point to the behavioral steps or pictures as a peer's role play unfolds) will be sufficient for the child to join in a role play at a later time.

STEP 5: SET UP THE ROLE PLAY

Following the discussion and listing of situations in which the skill is needed, a main actor is selected. The main actor chooses a second person (the coactor) to play the role of the other person (e.g., teacher, peer, parent) with whom he or she will use the skill in real life. The main actor should be encouraged to select as the coactor someone who resembles the significant other in as many ways as possible—in other words, someone who reminds the main actor most of the actual person.

The teacher then elicits from the main actor any additional information needed to set the stage for the role play. In order to make role-playing as realistic as possible, the teacher should obtain information as to where the problem will likely occur, what typically happens before the problem situation, and what attitude or manner the coactor should display. Props may be used if available and appropriate. We find it useful to assign separate behavioral steps to the observers, have them watch for the display of these steps, and then report on step use during the subsequent feedback session. For the first several role plays, observers can be coached as to what kinds of cues to observe (e.g., body language, words chosen, tone of voice, facial expression).

STEP 6: CONDUCT THE ROLE PLAY

At this point the teacher should remind group members of their roles: The main actor is to follow the behavioral steps and "think aloud" what would normally be thought silently; the coactor, to stay in the role of the other person; and the other students, to watch carefully for the portrayal of the behavioral steps.

The role players are then instructed to begin. At this point it is the teacher's responsibility to remind the main actor to "think out loud" and provide any help or coaching needed to keep the role play going according to the behavioral steps. If the role play is clearly going astray, the scene can be stopped, needed instruction provided, and the role play resumed. It is helpful for the teacher (or co-leader if one is available) to be positioned near the chalkboard or easel pad and to point to each of the steps as they are enacted. This will help the main actor, as well as the observers and coactor, follow the steps in order.

Role-playing should be continued until all group members have had an opportunity to participate as the main actor or until the attention of the group is waning. Sometimes giving everyone a chance will require two or more sessions for a given skill. As noted before, we suggest that each session begin with two modeling vignettes for the selected skill, even if the skill is not new to the group. It is important to note that, although the framework (behavioral steps) of each role play remains the same, the content can and should change from role play to role play. For example, even though several children may have difficulty with being teased on the playground, the situations in which they are teased, as well as the person who is the teaser, will be different. It is important for each child to role-play within the context of the real-life provocation.

Other strategies may be used to support a role play. For example, role reversal is often a useful procedure. If a student has a difficult time perceiving his or her coactor's point of view, having the two exchange roles and resume the role play can be most helpful. On occasion, the group leader can also assume the coactor role in an effort to give students the opportunity to handle types of reactions not otherwise role-played during the session. It may be critical to have a difficult adult role realistically portrayed, for instance. The leader as a coactor may also encourage less verbal or more hesitant students. The leader as coactor also may be indicated with particular skills (e.g., Dealing with Teasing, Skill 27), which otherwise would require the student coactor to engage in inappropriate or attention-getting behaviors.

STEP 7: PROVIDE PERFORMANCE FEEDBACK

A brief period of feedback follows each role play. Feedback lets the main actor find out how well he or she followed the behavioral steps, offers an evaluation of the impact of the role play on the coactor, and gives the main actor encouragement to try out the behavior in real life.

The coactor is typically asked to react first (e.g., "How did it feel when she said that to you?"). Next the observers comment on whether or not the skill steps they were assigned to watch for were followed and on other relevant aspects of the role play. Then the teacher or co-leader comments in particular on how well the behavioral steps were followed and provides social reinforcement (praise, approval, encouragement) for close following of the skill steps. To be most effective in providing reinforcement, the teacher should follow these guidelines:

- Provide reinforcement only after role plays that follow the behavioral steps.

- Provide reinforcement at the earliest appropriate opportunity after role plays that follow the behavioral steps.

- Provide reinforcement to the coactor for being helpful, cooperative, and so forth.

- Vary the specific content of the reinforcement offered (e.g., praise particular aspects of the performance, such as tone of voice, posture, phrasing).

- Provide reinforcement in an amount consistent with the quality of the role play.

In addition to following these guidelines, the teacher should provide enough role-playing activity for each group member to have sufficient opportunity to be reinforced. The teacher should not provide reinforcement when the role play departs significantly from the behavioral steps (except for "trying"). However, he or she may provide reinforcement for an individual student's improvement over previous performances and reteach the skill, if necessary.

After listening to the feedback from the coactor, observers, and group leaders, the main actor is asked to make comments regarding the role play and, if appropriate, to respond to the comments of others. In this way, the main actor can learn to evaluate the effectiveness of his or her skill performance in light of others' viewpoints.

In all aspects of feedback, group leaders must maintain the behavioral focus of Skillstreaming. Leader comments must point to the presence or absence of specific, concrete behaviors and not take the form of general evaluative comments or generalizations. Feedback, of course, may be positive or negative in content. Positive feedback should always be given first; otherwise, the child may be concentrating on the negative comments and not hear the other feedback. Negative feedback should be constructive in nature, offering suggestions for what might improve skill enactment. The group leader will need to model constructive comments before allowing young students to give this type of feedback to their peers. Whenever possible, children who fail to follow the behavioral steps in the role play should be given the opportunity to repeat the steps after receiving corrective, constructive criticism. At times, as a further feedback procedure, we have videotaped entire role plays. Giving students the opportunity to observe themselves on tape can be an effective aid, enabling them to reflect on their own behavior.

Because a primary goal of Skillstreaming is skill flexibility, role-play enactment that departs somewhat from the behavioral steps may not be "wrong." That is, a different approach to the skill may actually be effective in some situations. Teachers should stress that they are trying to teach effective choices and that learning the behavioral steps as shown will give children more choices for dealing with problems.

STEP 8: ASSIGN SKILL HOMEWORK

Following each successful role play (those in which the behavioral steps have been followed), the student is asked to try the skill in his or her own real-life setting. It is most helpful to begin with relatively simple homework assignments (e.g., situations that occur in the school environment, situations without a high level of stress or emotion) and, as mastery is achieved, work up to more complex and demanding assignments. This sequence provides the teacher with an opportunity to reinforce each approximation toward competent performance. The child should not be expected to perform the skill perfectly when first using it in real-life contexts. Reinforcement should be given as the child's performance comes closer to the ideal. Successful experiences when beginning to use the skill in the real world (i.e., successful completion of homework) and rewards received for doing so are critical in encouraging the student to attempt further use of the skill.

Two levels of homework are suggested. The first is used until the teacher is reasonably certain the child has a good understanding of the expected performance of the skill. The child can then be instructed to practice the skill by completing the second level of homework.

Homework Level 1

At this beginning level, the child thinks of a situation either at home or school in which he or she would like to or needs to practice the skill. When Skillstreaming is still fairly new to the group, the teacher may need to provide strong guidance in selecting these situations. It is especially helpful if the situation chosen is the same one the child has role-played successfully. On the Homework 1 Report (see Figure 2 for an example), the teacher lists the child's name, the date the assignment is made, the name of the skill the child will use, and the appropriate skill steps and illustrations. Together, the teacher and the child decide on the person with whom the child will try the skill and when the attempt will be made (e.g., during free play, outside at home after school). The child or the teacher should illustrate these decisions on the homework report in picture format. After the child actually tries the skill, the child evaluates how well he or she followed the steps by coloring in one of the three faces on the form. Because many young children may not be able to make accurate self-evaluations when they first begin this procedure, the teacher should discuss the child's reasons for the choice. In addition, it must be made clear to the child that this evaluation pertains to how well the skill steps were followed rather than how well the skill worked.

FIGURE 2　Homework 1 Report

Name ___Cory_____ Date _10/10/02_____

Skill ____Joining In (#15)_____

STEPS

1. Move closer.

2. Watch.

3. Ask.

Who?

Juan

When? Recess

How I did

Homework Level 2

The child who has been successful with Homework 1 assignments is ready to attempt monitoring his or her own skill use. With assistance from the child, the teacher completes the relevant information on the Homework 2 Report (see example in Figure 3), including the behavioral skill steps and illustrations for the target skill. Then, throughout the course of the day, the child colors a happy face whenever the skill is practiced.

Using the Homework Reports

The first part of each Skillstreaming session is devoted to presenting and discussing the children's homework assignments, which the teacher has previously reviewed on an individual basis. This individual review is suggested so that a child who may have been unsuccessful can be spared the possible embarrassment of sharing this failure publicly. When children have made an effort to complete their homework assignments, the teacher provides social reinforcement for this achievement. A child who repeatedly fails to complete the homework is likely to need further skill instruction, an opportunity to complete homework in a school setting that will allow the teacher to prompt the child, or more potent reinforcers (i.e., tangible rewards).

Group Rewards, Self-Monitoring Forms, Reinforcers, and Awards

Self-monitoring forms like the one shown in Figure 4 can help children follow through with skill practice, as can group reward forms (see the example in Figure 5). Skill tickets and notes like the examples in Figure 6 and Figure 7 can likewise motivate continued skill use. The Program Forms book supplements this text by including a variety of different self-recording forms and awards. Suggestions for using such materials to enhance skill generalization are given in chapter 8.

STEP 9: SELECT THE NEXT ROLE PLAYER

The next student is selected to serve as the main actor, and the sequence just described is repeated until all members of the Skillstreaming group or class are reliably demonstrating proficiency

FIGURE 3 Homework 2 Report

Name _____Elizabeth_____ Date ___10/10/02_____

Skill _____Dealing with Feeling Mad (#28)_____

STEPS

1. Stop and think.

2. Choose.

    a. Turtle.

    c. Relax.

    c. Ask to talk.

3. Do it.

How I did

FIGURE 4 **Self-Monitoring Form: Example 1**

Good for me!

Name _____ Rami _____

Date _____ 11/12/02 _____

Skill _____ Using Nice Talk (#2) _____

FIGURE 5   Group Reward Form

Together we can!

Skill _____ Listening (#1) _____

FIGURE 6 **Skill Ticket**

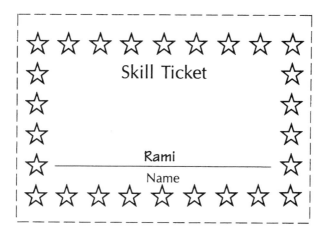

FIGURE 7 **Skill Note**

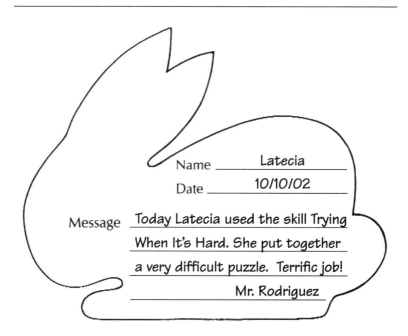

in using the skill. As noted previously, for young children opportunities for all to role-play successfully may require several Skillstreaming sessions on each skill.

SUMMARY

This chapter has presented the specific steps to follow in carrying out a Skillstreaming session with young children. These nine steps constitute the instructional sequence for teaching each of the skills included in Skillstreaming (chapter 6). Conditions that increase the effectiveness of instruction, as well as examples to illustrate how these steps are put into practice, have been described.

CHAPTER 5

A Sample Skillstreaming Session

This chapter presents an edited transcript of an introductory Skillstreaming session with children in a kindergarten classroom. The group consists of two leaders and ten students. This transcript depicts the leaders introducing students to what will happen in the group (as explained in chapter 3) and follows the Skillstreaming teaching procedures discussed in chapter 4. The skill used for instruction is Dealing with Teasing (Skill 27).

The goal of the introductory session for preschool and kindergarten children is to acquaint them with the concept of social skills, illustrate the activities that will be performed, and emphasize that, in this group, they will learn the things they want and need to learn. The following text suggests a typical format for this session. The teacher uses an easel pad to illustrate the Skillstreaming procedure and skill, and gives each student a Skill Card on which steps are written.

Introduction to Skillstreaming

Introductions

Introduce yourself and the other leader if the children do not know you. Ask the children to say their names if you or the other leader do not know the children or if the children do not know each other.

Explanation of prosocial skills and group purpose

Teacher: First of all, I'm going to tell you what we'll be learning the first thing in the morning every day. We're going to learn the things that you need and want to learn about getting along with friends and adults. How many of you like to play games? *(Children respond with "Me," "I do," or raised hands.)*

Teacher: Well, we're going to learn how to take turns so everybody has more fun in games. Taking turns is a social skill. Now, who likes to get in trouble? *(Children respond with "Not me," shaking their heads no.)* No, getting in trouble isn't much fun, is it? So we'll also learn ways to stay out of trouble, like what to do when you're mad or upset. And we'll all learn to be better friends with one another. These are all kinds of *social skills.* Do you think you'd like to learn these skills? *(Children respond in the affirmative.)*

Overview of Skillstreaming

Describe the four basic Skillstreaming procedures.

Teacher: First, we'll show you how to do a skill. *(modeling)*
Then you'll get to try it. *(role-playing)*
And we'll talk about how well you did. *(performance feedback)*
Then you'll get to practice it. *(generalization)*

Demonstrate for the group an example of learning another type of skill (i.e., self-help or academic skill).

Teacher: Let's say I want to learn how to tie my shoes. How am I going to learn to tie my shoes? *(Children respond with "Oh, you know," "Can't you tie your shoes?" etc.)*

Teacher: *(Holding up a large tennis shoe)* I need to learn how to tie my shoe. How will I learn this?

Jordan: Here, I'll show you.

Teacher: Terrific, Jordan. I'm going to need someone to show me how. I'm going to need to watch someone else. *(Writes "1. Watch" and draws two large eyes on the easel pad.)* That's the first part of learning a skill. What should I do next?

Lisa: You do it.

Teacher: You're absolutely right! I'm going to try it. *(Writes "2. Try" and draws a stick figure showing motion.)* Now, what if it's hard for me—what if I need some help?

Sammy: Jordan will tie it for you.

Teacher: OK, that's one good way, Sammy. That would be kind of Jordan, and I'd certainly get my shoe tied. But would I learn how to tie it myself? *(The group responds, "No.")*

Teacher: So what I need, then, is someone to tell me what I'm doing that's right and where I've messed up. Would that help me learn? *("Yes" and "Yeah" can be heard from the group. The teacher writes "3. Listen" and draws two large ears on the easel pad.)*

Teacher: Then once I've had someone tell me how to do it better, I'll need lots of practice, right? *(Writes "4. Practice" on the easel pad.)* This is the same way we'll learn social skills.

Explanation of the reinforcement system, if one will be used, and review of classroom rules

Teacher: *(Pulling a package from a bag)* Here I have lots of dinosaur stickers. Who likes dinosaurs? *(Group responds.)* I do! Well, for everyone who follows our classroom rules during social skills class and tries to learn the skills we're working on, I'll have a sticker for you to wear on your shirt at the end of the group. *(Note: Some groups or individual children may need a plan that gives positive reinforcement on a more frequent basis.)*

Conclusion

Teacher: We'll have fun learning these new social skills, and we'll help each other learn them. We may also have some special visitors come to the class—we'll have to wait and see!

Skill Instruction

Step 1: Define the skill

Teacher: Today we're going to learn a very important skill. It's called Dealing with Teasing *(Skill 27)*. What does the word *teasing* mean?

Enrique: Somebody tries to get you mad.

Sammy: They say mean things.

Ayul: They make fun of you, and you cry.

Cory: Or you hit them.

Savanah: My sister, she calls me "little creep." So I tell my mom.

Teacher: Those are good examples of teasing. Someone saying something mean, calling you a name, or in some way making fun of you are all examples of teasing. Some of you said you want to cry or hit the person who is teasing you, right? *(The children respond with nods and affirmative words.)* So being teased can result in your feeling sad or angry, right? *(Children respond.)* Well, it's OK to feel sad or angry when you're teased, but what will happen if you hit someone?

Ayul: You get yelled at.

Cory: I have to do a time-out.

Enrique: I miss recess.

Teacher: OK, then. Let's work on Dealing with Teasing so you don't have to cry or get into trouble by fighting back. Here are the steps to Dealing with Teasing. *(Shows and reads the steps written on the easel pad with corresponding pictures.)*

Dealing with Teasing

1. Stop and think.
2. Say, "Please stop."
3. Walk away.

Teacher: These three steps, in this order, make up a good way to deal with being teased. The first step is to tell yourself to stop so that you don't hit the person and get in trouble or cry. If you cry, the person will probably keep teasing you, right? *(Students respond.)* Yes, the person will know the teasing works—that it makes you very sad.

With the second step, saying, "Please stop," it's important to use a brave voice. Remember when we practiced Using Brave Talk (Skill 3)? The third step is walking away. Remember to walk away in a brave way, too.

Step 2: Model the skill

Teacher: Julia, our peer helper, is here today to help with modeling the skill of Dealing with Teasing. We'll show you how to follow each of the steps. While we show you, what is your job? *(Points to the word* watch *and the picture of the eyes.)* Right! Your job is to watch as Julia, first, stops and thinks about the problem. Then Julia will ask me to please stop. Then she'll walk away. Are you ready, Julia? *(Julia nods.)* We're on the playground, and Julia is playing by herself. I'll tease her, and we'll watch Julia follow the steps.

Teacher: *(Julia is holding a ball and tossing it gently; the teacher walks past her.)* Hey, little creep. What's a creep like you doing with that ball?

Julia: First I need to tell myself to stop and think. If I cry, she'll keep teasing me. If I hit her, I'll just get in trouble. I need to tell her to stop in a brave voice. *(Turns toward the teacher.)* Please stop. *(Turns away.)* Then I need to walk away. *(Walks away from the teacher.)*

Teacher: Did Julia follow the steps of the skill? Did she first stop and think? *(The children respond.)* Yes, you knew she did because she talked herself

through it. Did she follow the second step? Did
she say, "Please stop"? *(Children respond.)* And
did she follow the last step? Did she walk away?
(Children respond.) How did Julia do? Did she
follow all three steps? Good job! Thank you,
Julia. Now we'll show you another example.

(Julia and the teacher model another example.)

Step 3: Establish student skill need

Teacher: Let's think of some times when you are really
teased, and it's difficult for you to deal with.
I'll write your names on the easel pad and
your situation beside your name. Who can
think of a time when you are teased, and it's a
problem?

Sammy: When I play football with my friends. They laugh
at me.

Savannah: My sister calls me names.

Cory: On the bus, going home, the big kids call me
shrimp, and I'm not doing anything to have them
call me that.

Ayul: A girl says I look funny.

*(The listing continues as each child identifies a situa-
tion for skill use.)*

Step 4: Select the first role player

Teacher: You all came up with really good examples of
when you need to use the skill. Who would like
to role-play or try the skill first? OK, Ayul. The
girl who teases you really seems to be a problem
for you.

Step 5: Set up the role play

Teacher: Ayul, could you tell us a little more about what
happens?

Ayul: When I walk home, this bigger girl, I don't know her name, but she says I look stupid. She says I have fat lips. *(Starts to cry.)*

Teacher: Ayul, this skill will help you get her to stop, OK? Will you work with us to learn how to handle this so she'll stop? *(Ayul nods.)* Great! Let's start. I tell you what, Ayul. How about I pretend first to be the girl who teases you? *(Ayul agrees.)*

I think we have a good idea of what happens. Before we start with the role play, I'm going to ask each of you to watch the role play carefully. I want each of you to watch for a certain step. Enrique, John, and Hannah, will you watch to see if Ayul does the first step? See if she stops and thinks? Sammy, Rami, and Joel, will you watch for the second step? See if Ayul says, "Please stop"? And Savannah, Cory, and Marcus, will you watch for the third step? Will you watch for Ayul to walk away?

Teacher: Ayul, look at your Skill Card with the skill steps. The pictures will help you remember. First, you'll say something like "I have to stop and think." This is to give you some time. Then you'll say, "Please stop," in a brave way. The third step is to walk away. Remember, we'll help you if you want. Are you ready? *(Ayul nods.)*

Step 6: Conduct the role play

Teacher: OK, Ayul, you're walking home from school. Here's your backpack. This chair will be at the corner where the older girl teases you. *(Ayul puts on her backpack and starts to walk across the room.)*

Teacher: *(In a taunting voice)* Hey, you, funny-looking girl. You sure look funny.

Ayul: *(Stops.)*

Teacher: The first step is to stop and think. Ayul, say it out loud so we know you're thinking this.

Ayul: I have to stop and think. I won't be sad.

Teacher: Good. Now, what's the next step? You can look at your card.

Ayul: *(Turning to the teacher)* Please stop.

Teacher: Good. Next, what will you do?

Ayul: *(Looking at her card, Ayul walks off with her head held high.)*

Teacher: Good for you, Ayul!

Ayul: *(Smiles.)*

Step 7: Provide performance feedback

Teacher: Ayul, if I were the girl teasing you, I think I'd pick on someone else instead. I don't think I got you upset! Let's check out what the group saw. *(Puts her arm around Ayul.)* Did Ayul do the first step? Did she stop and think? *(The children nod.)* How do you know?

John: Ayul said stop and think.

Teacher: Good watching! We heard her think this out loud! Did Ayul follow the second step? Did she say, "Please stop"?

Joel: Yeah.

Teacher: Yes, she did. Did she say this in a brave way? *(The children nod.)* Yes, she wasn't shy or angry. Good. And the third step?

Marcus: She walked away.

Teacher: Thank you, Marcus. She did walk away. You all did a terrific job watching! Ayul, how did it feel to use this skill?

Ayul: Good.

Teacher: Was it hard to do?

Ayul: Kinda.

Teacher: Sure. Dealing with teasing is difficult! Ayul, you're off to a great start in really using this skill on your way home from school! Good for you— you did it!

Step 8: Assign skill homework

Teacher: Ayul, after the group, let's plan out a homework assignment, a time when you can try out the skill, OK? *(Ayul agrees. Note: To increase the like-lihood that Ayul will be successful in using the skill with the real-life provocation on her way home from school, the teacher will coach Ayul again before asking her to try it.)*

Step 9: Select the next role player

Teacher: Who would like to try the skill next?

CHAPTER 6

Skills for Preschool and Kindergarten Students

This chapter presents the Skillstreaming curriculum, a set of 40 skills designed to enhance the prosocial development of preschool and kindergarten children. These skills are divided into six skill groups:

1. Beginning Social Skills, which are most easily learned by the young child and often are prerequisites to later skill acquisition and instruction

2. School-Related Skills, which enhance success primarily in the school or early childhood environment

3. Friendship-Making Skills, which encourage positive peer interaction

4. Dealing with Feelings, skills designed to foster awareness of the feelings of self and others

5. Alternatives to Aggression, skills that provide the child with prosocial choices in dealing with conflict

6. Dealing with Stress, skills that address the stressful situations frequently encountered by young children

As defined by Gresham (1998), "Social skills are defined as socially acceptable learned behaviors enabling individuals to interact effectively with others and avoid or escape socially unacceptable behaviors exhibited by others" (p. 20).

The skills in this curriculum, listed in Table 2, involve those social behaviors believed to be related to peer acceptance (Dodge, 1983; Greenwood, Todd, Hops, & Walker, 1982; Mize & Ladd, 1984), positive teacher attention (Cartledge & Milburn, 1980), and social competence (Spivack & Shure, 1974), as well as those likely to enhance children's personal satisfaction (Goldstein & McGinnis, 1997). Additional prosocial skills have been selected to teach alternatives to the maladaptive behaviors often employed by unpopular or rejected children, such as poor cooperation (Coie & Kupersmidt, 1983), anxiety (Buhremester, 1982), disruptive behaviors (Dodge, Coie, & Bralke, 1982), and verbal and physical aggression (Dodge et al., 1982). The selection of social skills for instruction needs to be based on the child's individual characteristics (e.g., developmental level, cognitive and behavioral deficits) and on social criteria (e.g., cultural context, situational specificity, peer relationships, social validity; Cartledge & Milburn, 1995).

This list of prosocial behaviors is by no means all-inclusive; instead, our goal is to provide teachers and others who recognize skill or performance deficits in young children with detailed lesson plans to teach the behavioral skills typically needed by preschool and kindergarten children. As the person who implements these plans observes concerns in the school and play environments, and as parents and children express difficulties, new skills can and should be developed. For example, although Asking a Question (Skill 9) is intended to encompass asking permission as well, the teacher who finds problems pertaining to asking permission to be frequent may choose to designate and develop this behavior as a separate prosocial skill. In addition, when the individual needs of the children and the circumstances of the setting are considered, it may be that a given skill will be retained but that one or more of the behavioral steps will need to be altered or deleted to achieve the best outcome. Teachers and other group leaders should use their experience and judgment in adjusting the content of these skills.

TABLE 2 **Skillstreaming Curriculum for Preschool and Kindergarten Children**

Group I: Beginning Social Skills

1. Listening
2. Using Nice Talk
3. Using Brave Talk
4. Saying Thank You
5. Rewarding Yourself
6. Asking for Help
7. Asking a Favor
8. Ignoring

Group II: School-Related Skills

9. Asking a Question
10. Following Directions
11. Trying When It's Hard
12. Interrupting

Group III: Friendship-Making Skills

13. Greeting Others
14. Reading Others
15. Joining In
16. Waiting Your Turn
17. Sharing
18. Offering Help
19. Asking Someone to Play
20. Playing a Game

Group IV: Dealing with Feelings

21. Knowing Your Feelings
22. Feeling Left Out
23. Asking to Talk
24. Dealing with Fear
25. Deciding How Someone Feels
26. Showing Affection

Group V: Alternatives to Aggression

27. Dealing with Teasing
28. Dealing with Feeling Mad
29. Deciding If It's Fair
30. Solving a Problem
31. Accepting Consequences

Group VI: Dealing with Stress

32. Relaxing
33. Dealing with Mistakes
34. Being Honest
35. Knowing When to Tell
36. Dealing with Losing
37. Wanting to Be First
38. Saying No
39. Accepting No
40. Deciding What to Do

Skill 1: Listening

STEPS

1. Look.

Discuss the importance of looking at the person who is talking. Point out that sometimes you may think someone isn't listening, even though he or she really is. These steps are to show someone that you are really listening.

2. Stay still.

Remind the children that staying still means keeping hands and feet still and not talking with friends.

3. Think.

Encourage the children to think about what the person is saying, and be sure they understand if the person is asking them to do something.

SUGGESTED SITUATIONS

School: Your teacher tells you that you are to go to the art center; your teacher gives you instructions on how to do an activity.

Home: A parent is telling you plans for the weekend.

Peer group: A friend is telling you a story.

COMMENTS

This is a good skill with which to begin your Skillstreaming group. Adults often tell young children to listen without explaining the specific behaviors or steps necessary to do so. Once the skill of listening is learned, it can be incorporated into classroom rules. Giving the children a special cue to listen (e.g., "Do you have your listening ears on?") may help them apply the skill when needed.

Play the listening game of Simon Says.

Have students listen to follow the directions to complete a drawing.

In small groups, have students listen to complete a cooperative drawing or group project.

Skill 2: Using Nice Talk

STEPS

1. Use a friendly look.

Discuss how your body and facial expressions can give a friendly or unfriendly look. You may want to act out different facial expressions and body postures to help the children identify what is friendly.

2. Use a friendly voice.

Tell the children that a friendly voice is an "inside" voice—not loud like they might use outside, angry, or whining. Again, you may wish to act out different voice tones and volumes and have the children identify which ones are friendly.

SUGGESTED SITUATIONS

School: A teacher asks you to do a favor.

Home: A parent has just reminded you to pick up your toys.

Peer group: A friend is playing with the toy you wanted.

COMMENTS

This skill is intended to be used with other skills that require a verbal response. The children can be helped to understand that often it's not so much what is said as the way it is said that may elicit an angry response. Once children have learned this skill, reminding them to use nice talk can reduce the frequency of loud talking and/or whining.

RELATED SKILL-SUPPORTING ACTIVITY

Make a chart titled "Using Nice Talk." During free play, circulate around the classroom. When a student talks in an unfriendly or angry way, quietly take the child aside and prompt him or her to use "nice talk." When the student uses the skill, put a smiley-face sticker on the chart. Provide a total class special activity when the chart is filled with stickers.

Skill 3: Using Brave Talk

STEPS

1. When?
Discuss situations in which children should use a brave (i.e., assertive) response.

2. Use a brave look.
Discuss body posture and facial expressions that convey a brave look. Distinguish this look from an angry look (e.g., clenching teeth) and a friendly look (e.g., smiling).

3. Use a brave voice.
Discuss that a brave voice is one slightly louder than a friendly one and in which the words are spoken more clearly. Show examples of this voice versus friendly and angry voices.

SUGGESTED SITUATIONS

School: A friend keeps pressuring you to take one of the school toys home with you.

Home: A brother or sister encourages you to draw a picture on the outside of the house with markers.

Peer group: A friend wants you both to play in your parents' car.

COMMENTS

Another situation in which children could use this skill is when an older peer urges them to behave in ways that make them feel uncomfortable (e.g., crossing the street when they aren't supposed to). The use of puppets may help to lessen the anxiety when children are role-playing such situations.

RELATED SKILL-SUPPORTING ACTIVITY

Show different expressions and tones of voice to the children by using pictures, videotapes, and/or performing the actions live. Have the children hold up cards to indicate whether the actions are friendly, brave, or angry.

Skill 4: Saying Thank You

STEPS

1. Was it nice to do?

Talk about nice things that parents, teachers, and friends do for others. Tell the children that saying thank you is a way to let someone know you are happy about what that person did for you.

2. When?

Discuss appropriate times to say thank you (i.e., when the person isn't busy).

3. Say, "Thank you."

Let the children know that they may want to tell the person why they are saying thank you (e.g., that they really wanted that toy or that something the person did made them feel good), especially if they must thank the person later.

SUGGESTED SITUATIONS

School: Someone gives you a school toy that you wanted.

Home: A parent fixes your favorite dinner.

Peer group: A friend invites you to a birthday party; a friend lets you play with a special toy.

COMMENTS

If children have already learned Using Nice Talk (Skill 2), they can be reminded to use it when they are saying thanks.

RELATED SKILL-SUPPORTING ACTIVITIES

Generate with the children other ways to say thank you, such as smiling, giving a hug, or doing something nice for the person.

Practice different ways of saying thank you, such as "That was nice of you to do for me" or "I felt good when you said that to me."

Develop a "thank you" list of people within the school who have helped students. Each week, plan a way to thank one of the people on that list (e.g., make a card or banner; write a note and tuck it inside a balloon, then blow up the balloon and give it to the person).

Skill 5: Rewarding Yourself

STEPS

1. How did you do?

Discuss ways of evaluating one's own performance. These might include feeling as
though something was hard but that you
tried, hearing someone else praise your
efforts, or having a good feeling inside
about how you did.

2. Say, "Good for me!"

Discuss the feeling of being proud of
yourself. Have the children talk about
times when they have felt this way. Give
examples of other things they might say
to reward themselves (e.g., "Way to go,"
"I really did a good job").

SUGGESTED SITUATIONS

School: You helped the teacher or another child; you did a good
job on an activity.

Home: You cleaned up your room; you helped clear the table.

Peer group: You helped a friend learn how to play a game.

COMMENTS

Emphasize that a person doesn't always have to depend on others
to reward his or her actions.

RELATED SKILL-SUPPORTING ACTIVITY

If the group is large, divide into smaller groups of four to six students each. Have the children take turns telling one thing they
did well that day. Have the children reward themselves (e.g., say,
"Good for me," or give themselves a pat on the back). Each day,
write a note to several parents about their children's achievement. Be sure at the end of the week that all children have had an
"I did it" note to take home.

Skill 6: Asking for Help

STEPS

1. Try it.

Talk about the importance of trying on your own first. Sometimes people ask for help instead of trying something difficult by themselves, but doing something difficult on your own can give you a feeling of pride.

2. Say, "I need help."

Acknowledge that sometimes it's frustrating when something is difficult to do, but stress the importance of Using Nice Talk (Skill 2).

SUGGESTED SITUATIONS

School: You need help putting the paints back up on the shelf.

Home: You need help from a parent in getting dressed for school or finding your swimming suit.

Peer group: You want to ask a friend to help you learn to ride your bike.

COMMENTS

Remind the children that they may want to use the skill of Saying Thank You (Skill 4) after the help is given. This will help the child understand how to use a sequence of prosocial skills.

Have children list and/or illustrate the activities or skills each is particularly good at. Discuss individual differences; stress that it is OK to ask for help if it's needed. These lists may also stimulate the children to ask for help from peers who have listed certain areas as strengths.

Create a classroom "yellow pages," which lists strengths or services (e.g., math skills, playing a certain board game, tying shoes). (Be sure each child has his or her name in the pages at least once!) Encourage students to look in the yellow pages if they need help with something.

Skill 7: Asking a Favor

STEPS

1. What do you want?
Explain that this skill may be used to express children's wants or needs but that the favor should be a fair one. Deciding If It's Fair (Skill 29) will help them determine this.

2. Plan what to say.
Talk about the importance of planning what to say and suggest several possible ways to ask. The children may also want to give a reason for asking the favor (e.g., "Could you please move a little? I can't see when you sit there").

3. Ask.

4. Say, "Thank you."
Refer to Saying Thank You (Skill 4).

SUGGESTED SITUATIONS

School: You want to use the markers another child is using.

Home: You ask your parent to make popcorn.

Peer group: You want to ride a friend's bicycle.

COMMENTS

Once the children have been successful in using this skill in role-play situations, it is particularly important that they practice what to do when the favor isn't granted. Adding the statement "Thanks anyway" or having the child get involved in something else may be helpful.

RELATED SKILL-SUPPORTING ACTIVITY

Make a list of favors that would be fair and those that would not. For example, if a person has a pack of gum, would it be fair to ask for a stick? If a person has one stick of gum, would it be fair to ask for it?

Skill 8: Ignoring

STEPS

1. Look away.

Tell the children not to look at the person they want to avoid. They can turn their heads away, look at a friend, or pick up a book or toy to look at.

2. Close your ears.

Tell children not to listen to what the annoying person is saying. If they are supposed to be listening to someone else (such as a teacher), they can listen to that person.

3. Be quiet.

Remind children not to say anything back to the person who is annoying.

SUGGESTED SITUATIONS

School: Another child is talking when you are supposed to be listening to the teacher.

Home: A brother or sister is trying to keep you from listening to your CD.

Peer group: Another child is trying to interfere with a game you are playing.

COMMENTS

Discuss that sometimes someone who is acting silly is trying to get attention. A good way to teach that person not to act silly is to avoid giving him any attention at all. Also discuss the idea that sometimes friends will bother others because they really want to play, too. In this case, the children may want to ask the child to join in. Finally, talk about other ways of ignoring, such as leaving the room (at home) or getting involved in another activity (at school).

Tell the class that during this class activity, one that they are to do independently at their work stations, you will walk around the room and try to distract them. They are to practice Ignoring. Be sure each child has a copy of the steps of the skill to serve as a reminder.

In pairs, have one child tell what he or she did last night. First, have the other child listen to what is being said. (It may be necessary to review Skill 1, Listening.) Next have the child tell again what he or she did, directing the other child to use the skill of Ignoring. As a group, discuss how it felt to be listened to and how it felt to be ignored.

Skill 9: Asking a Question

STEPS

1. **What to ask?**
   Discuss what children need to ask and how to decide whether the question is really necessary. Help them plan out what they need to ask.

2. **Whom to ask?**
   Discuss how to decide if they should ask the teacher, a parent, or someone else.

3. **When to ask?**
   Talk about how to choose a good time to ask (i.e., when the other person isn't busy).

4. **Ask.**
   Stress the importance of Using Nice Talk (Skill 2).

SUGGESTED SITUATIONS

School: You want to ask your teacher about when the field trip is; you want to ask to use the markers and glue.

Home: You want to ask a parent if you can visit a friend.

Peer group: You want to ask a friend if she would like to play at your house; you want to ask how a friend made something.

COMMENTS

Young children often phrase questions as statements. Modeling the question form when such situations arise will help them learn an alternate way of expressing themselves.

Practice asking questions via a game format. For example, make a statement such as "I want a glass of milk," and ask the children to change the statement to a question ("May I have a glass of milk?").

State a topic (e.g., swimming) and, as a group, generate several questions that could be asked about that topic. Discourage questions unrelated to the topic.

Skill 10: Following Directions

STEPS

1. Listen.

Review Listening (Skill 1). Discuss the importance of having children show that they are listening.

2. Think about it.

Remind the children to think about what is being said.

3. Ask if needed.

Encourage children to ask questions about anything they don't understand. (Review or teach Skill 9, Asking a Question).

4. Do it.

SUGGESTED SITUATIONS

School: Your teacher gives you the directions to do some work at a learning center.

Home: A parent gives you directions to make a snack.

Peer group: A friend tells you how to play a game.

COMMENTS

Sometimes directions given to young children are too complex for them to complete successfully. Give directions consisting of only one or two steps until the children are familiar with following directions. It's helpful to preface a direction with a consistent cue, such as "Here's the direction."

Play the Treasure Hunt game, giving the children verbal directions to find a special treat or activity (e.g., "Walk to the bookshelf and look on the bottom shelf under the big book").

Read the book *Strega Nona,* by Tomie de Paola (Simon and Schuster, 1979). Discuss the consequences in this story when Big Anthony didn't follow directions. Discuss the consequences of not following directions in the children's own lives.

Skill 11: Trying When It's Hard

STEPS

1. Stop and think.
Discuss the feeling of frustration, and point out that lots of people get frustrated when something is difficult.

2. Say, "It's hard, but I'll try."
Talk about feeling proud when something is hard but you try it anyway. Also stress that it's OK to try and fail.

3. Try it.
Point out that a person might need to try more than once.

SUGGESTED SITUATIONS

School: Your teacher gives you an assignment that you don't think you can do.

Home: A parent wants you to do a chore that you don't think you can do (e.g., make the beds).

Peer group: A friend wants you to roller blade with him, but you think it's too hard.

COMMENTS

For the child who is afraid of failure, this will be a particularly valuable skill. Reinforce the idea that the only way to learn new things is to try those that are difficult. When assigning pre-academic or academic skills, be sure that tasks asked of the children are ones they are capable of completing with effort.

RELATED SKILL-SUPPORTING ACTIVITY

Read *The Little Engine That Could,* by Watty Piper (Platt and Munk, 1976), and discuss the feelings of each of the characters in the story. Also discuss what might have happened if the little engine didn't try. Substitute stories with similar themes, such as *The Little Red Ant and the Great Big Crumb: A Mexican Fable,* by Shirley Climo (Clarion, 1999).

Skill 12: Interrupting

STEPS

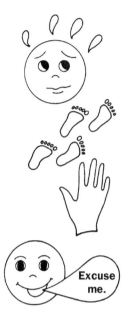

1. Decide if you need to.

Discuss when it is appropriate to inter-rupt (i.e., when you need help but the person you want to talk to isn't looking at you).

2. Walk to the person.

3. Wait.

Emphasize the importance of waiting without talking. Tell children to wait until the person stops talking and looks at you.

4. Say, "Excuse me."

Discuss how to know the person is ready to hear you (e.g., the person looks at you). The children can then ask what they need to.

SUGGESTED SITUATIONS

School: Your teacher is talking with another adult, and you need help with your activity.

Home: A parent is talking on the telephone, and you want to ask whether you can go outside.

Peer group: Your friend is talking with another person, and you want to ask whether you can play with your friend's wagon.

COMMENTS

It will be important to discuss situations in which children should not interrupt (i.e., to ask a question that could wait) and situations in which they should interrupt immediately (i.e., in an emergency). It may be helpful to have the children actually say to the adult, "This is an emergency" when such cases arise.

Provide pictures of a variety of situations and, as a group, have the children put the pictures under one of the following headings: "Do Not Interrupt," "OK to Interrupt," or "Emergency."

Skill 13: Greeting Others

STEPS

1. **Smile.**

2. **Say, "Hi, ."**
   Encourage children to use the person's
   name if they know it.

3. **Walk on.**
   This step should be used if the children
   are supposed to be following along with
   the group or if they don't know the person well. The children may wish to begin
   a conversation if the person is a friend
   and if it is an OK time to have a conversation.

SUGGESTED SITUATIONS

School: You pass by the school secretary in the hallway.

Home: A friend of your parents is visiting.

Peer group: Another child is walking past your house with her
parents.

COMMENTS

This skill is intended for use with people the child knows only
casually or in situations in which starting a conversation would
likely be inappropriate.

RELATED SKILL-SUPPORTING ACTIVITY

With the children, take a walk around the school and practice
greeting others.

Skill 14: Reading Others

STEPS

1. Look at the face.

Discuss the importance of watching for different facial expressions, such as smiling, frowning, clenching teeth together, and so forth.

2. Look at the body.

Talk about the feelings shown in a person's body position, such as putting head down, making fists with hands, placing hands on hips, and so on.

SUGGESTED SITUATIONS

School: The teacher walks in the class and smiles, or she has her hands on her hips and frowns.

Home: A parent is sitting with his head resting on his hands and not saying anything.

Peer group: A friend keeps turning away from you and doesn't answer you when you try to talk.

COMMENTS

For some children, paying attention to nonverbal communication (facial expressions and body posture) will be quite difficult, and considerable practice with this skill will be necessary.

RELATED SKILL-SUPPORTING ACTIVITIES

Show a variety of pictures of people engaged in everyday activities. (These pictures can be cut from magazines.) Have children describe the facial expressions and body postures shown in the pictures.

When reading picture books to the class, draw attention to the characters' facial expressions and body postures as clues to how the characters might feel.

Skill 15: Joining In

STEPS

1. Move closer.
Point out that the children should be fairly close to where the activity is taking place.

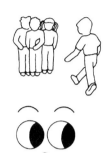

2. Watch.
Tell the children to watch the ongoing activity and wait for a pause. Discuss the importance of choosing a time to follow through with the next step (i.e., before the activity has begun or when there is a break in the activity).

3. Ask.
Suggest possible things to say, such as "That looks fun! Could I play, too?" Stress the importance of Using Brave Talk (Skill 3).

SUGGESTED SITUATIONS

School: You want to join in a game at recess or during free play.

Home: You want to play a game with a brother, sister, or parent.

Peer group: You want to join a group of children at the park.

COMMENTS

Research indicates that attempts to join in are more successful if the child hovers near the ongoing activity before asking to join in (Dodge, Schlundt, Schoken, & Dehugach, 1983). Children may need to use alternative skills if they are repeatedly rejected by a certain peer group. Practice in Reading Others (Skill 14) may help them assess other children's receptivity to such overtures.

RELATED SKILL-SUPPORTING ACTIVITY

During free play in the classroom or on the playground, tell the children that they will be practicing this skill. For each activity, review the steps with three or four children, then have them try out the skill. Discuss the outcomes with the class.

Skill 16: Waiting Your Turn

STEPS

1. **Say, "It's hard to wait, but I can do it."**
   Discuss how the children feel when they have to wait.

It's hard but I can.

2. **Choose.**

   a. **Wait quietly.**
      Discuss that this choice means not talking or bothering anyone else and remembering not to get angry or frustrated.

   b. **Do something else.**
      Talk about what things the children could do while they are waiting.

3. **Do it.**
   Children should make one of these choices.

   GO

SUGGESTED SITUATIONS

School: You are waiting your turn to play a game or to use the playground equipment.

Home: You are waiting until it's time for you to go to a movie or to the park.

Peer group: You are waiting your turn to have a toy.

COMMENTS

Remember to use a coping model during the modeling displays, because this skill can be a difficult one for the young child, who may be impulsive.

RELATED SKILL-SUPPORTING ACTIVITY

To practice this skill, as well as to show the group a product resulting from working together and taking turns, structure round-robin activities in the classroom, such as cooperatively making a collage, putting together a puzzle, or making a card or banner as a thank-you for someone. If the group is large, three or four groups could be completing the activity simultaneously. Remind the children to use the skill (post the steps or give each child a Skill Card).

Skill 17: Sharing

STEPS

1. Make a sharing plan.

Discuss the different plans children could make, such as playing with a toy together or having each child take a turn with the toy for a set period of time.

2. Ask.

Remind the children of the importance of Using Nice Talk (Skill 2) when asking friends if they agree to the plan.

3. Do it.

Talk about the importance of following through with the plan until a different plan is decided upon.

SUGGESTED SITUATIONS

School: You have to share the glue and other art materials with two other children.

Home: You must share the last cookie with a brother or sister.

Peer group: You have to share your toys with a friend who has come to your house to play.

COMMENTS

It is appropriate to discuss how the children feel when someone doesn't share with them and to encourage them to think about their feelings when someone asks them to share.

RELATED SKILL-SUPPORTING ACTIVITIES

Plan activities to encourage this skill, such as sharing art materials, taking turns when cooking, or engaging in other cooperative activities.

Divide children into groups of four or five at each table. Instruct each child to complete his or her own art activity. However, provide only one or two pair of scissors and glue containers for each table. Remind the students to use the skill of Sharing.

Skill 18: Offering Help

STEPS

1. Decide if someone needs help.
Discuss how to tell when someone might want or need help (e.g., someone has lots to carry or is showing frustration).

2. Ask.
Discuss appropriate ways of asking, such as saying, "May I help you?" or "How can I help you?"

3. Do it.
Discuss what to do if the person does not want your help.

SUGGESTED SITUATIONS

School: Your teacher looks frustrated while trying to pass out snacks and help a child who is upset at the same time.

Home: A parent is hurrying to get dinner ready.

Peer group: A friend is having trouble getting her coat on.

COMMENTS

Discuss what to do if the person doesn't want the help (e.g., walk away, get involved in another activity, say to yourself, "I did a good job asking" or "It was nice of me to ask").

RELATED SKILL-SUPPORTING ACTIVITIES

Include this skill when teaching units on community helpers by asking the people who come in to talk to the class to discuss ways they offer help to others.

Generate a class list of ways the children could help someone at home. Ask students to follow through with one of these suggestions. (Having the children draw a picture of what they plan to do, then take the picture home, will serve as a reminder.)

Skill 19: Asking Someone to Play

STEPS

1. Decide if you want to.

Discuss how to decide whether you want someone to play with or you would rather play alone. Point out that there might be times when you would rather be alone.

2. Decide who.

Talk about whom the child might choose (e.g., someone who is playing alone, someone new in the class the child would like to get to know, someone who isn't busy).

3. Ask.

Discuss and practice ways to ask (e.g., "Do you want to play?" or "Will you play this with me?")

SUGGESTED SITUATIONS

School: You want to play with someone when it's free play time.

Home: You want to ask a brother, sister, or parent to play.

Peer group: You want to play with a friend in the neighborhood.

COMMENTS

It is important to point out that it is best to ask someone to play after the person has finished his or her work at school or at home.

RELATED SKILL-SUPPORTING ACTIVITY

Write each child's name on a small index card or sheet of paper. During free play, have or four children draw a name. This is the child they will ask to play. (You may have to guide the children in an activity that they both would enjoy.)

Skill 20: Playing a Game

STEPS

1. Know the rules.

Discuss that everyone playing should agree on the rules before the game begins.

2. Who goes first?

Talk about ways to decide, such as rolling a die or offering to let the other person go first.

3. Wait for a turn.

Emphasize the importance of paying attention to the game and watching and waiting for your own turn.

SUGGESTED SITUATIONS

School: You are practicing shooting baskets at recess with two other friends.

Home: You are playing a board game with your mom.

Peer group: You are playing school with a friend.

COMMENTS

Two good skills to teach along with this one are Dealing with Losing (Skill 36) and Wanting to Be First (Skill 37).

RELATED SKILL-SUPPORTING ACTIVITY

Provide opportunities for the children to play board games in pairs or small groups, emphasizing use of this skill. Teach a variety of games children may play at recess or during free play in the classroom.

Skill 21: Knowing Your Feelings

STEPS

1. **Think about what happened.**
   Discuss what happened that may have
   caused the feeling. Also talk about the
   signals the children's bodies give that
   indicate they are having a strong feeling.

2. **Decide on the feeling.**
   Discuss a variety of feelings, such
   as anger, happiness, frustration,
   fear, and so on.

3. **Say, " I feel _____."**

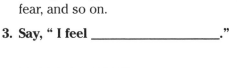

SUGGESTED SITUATIONS

School: You have to go to a new school where you don't know any
of the kids.

Home: Your parent announces that the whole family is going to a
movie that you had been wanting to see.

Peer group: You didn't get invited to a friend's birthday party.

COMMENTS

Explore as many different feeling words as the children can handle, trying to expand their vocabulary beyond the typical feelings
of happy, sad, and mad.

RELATED SKILL-SUPPORTING ACTIVITIES

Read the story *I Was So Mad,* by Mercer Mayer (Western, 1983).
Discuss how the main character's body might feel during different
parts of the story.

Read the book *Feelings,* by Aliki (William Morrow, 1986). Discuss
times when the children have had similar feelings. Ask how they
knew (how their bodies felt) when they were having those feelings.

Present pictures of people and animals, and help children identify
what feelings may be expressed. Generate ideas as to what may
have caused these feelings.

Skill 22: Feeling Left Out

STEPS

1. Decide what happened.

Discuss situations in which the children may feel left out and help them decide what caused them to feel this way. Talk about reasons why someone may not be included (e.g., a friend could only invite three people to her birthday party).

2. Choose.

a. Join in.

Children may need prior instruction in Joining In (Skill 15).

b. Do something else.

Generate ideas for other things children could do. Suggest that they may want to invite a friend to do one of these activities.

3. Do it.

Children should make one of these choices.

SUGGESTED SITUATIONS

School: You are left out of a game during free play.

Home: Your sister won't let you come into her room.

Peer group: A friend has invited someone else to go skating.

COMMENTS

The children may need practice in Reading Others (Skill 14) or Deciding How Someone Feels (Skill 25) in order to assess whether or not the other child or group of children is approachable.

Discuss the types of feelings that result from being left out, such as anger, hurt, loneliness, or frustration.

Read the story *Alejandro's Gift,* by Richard Albert (Chronicle Publishing, 1996). Discuss how Alejandro felt and what he did about it.

Skill 23: Asking to Talk

STEPS

1. Decide if you need to talk.
Discuss times when something might bother children and they might want to talk to someone about it.

2. Who?
Decide whom to talk with (i.e., a parent, teacher, or friend).

3. When?
Decide when would be a good time to ask (i.e., when the person isn't busy with something or someone else).

4. Say, "I need to talk."
Stress the importance of Using Nice Talk (Skill 2) to say this.

SUGGESTED SITUATIONS

School: You are feeling sad because you didn't have a turn at the painting center.

Home: Your parent bought your brother something that you had wanted.

Peer group: You feel that a friend would rather play with someone other than you.

COMMENTS

Stress that everyone experiences problems at some time and, although talking with someone may not actually solve the problem, it will likely help make you feel better anyway.

Write descriptions of times when talking with someone would be helpful (include the situations generated by the students during initial instruction in this skill). Have the children, in turn, draw a card on which one of these situations has been listed. (Depending upon the reading skills of the class, it may be necessary to select a reader from the class or to read the situations yourself.) Ask each child whom he or she would ask to talk with, and follow through by role-playing the skill.

Skill 24: Dealing with Fear

STEPS

1. What?

Discuss situations that cause children to be afraid.

2. Choose.

    a. Ask to talk.

       Refer to Asking to Talk (Skill 23).

    b. Relax.

       Refer to Relaxing (Skill 32).

3. Do it.

Children should make one of these choices.

SUGGESTED SITUATIONS

School: A parent is late, and you're afraid he or she isn't coming.

Home: A brother or sister is watching a scary movie.

Peer group: You are afraid to go out of the house because an older child said he would get you.

COMMENTS

Discuss that there are events in which a real danger is present and fear is appropriate. Many other situations, such as being afraid of the dark, are quite normal for this age group and likely present no serious problems for most children. However, explain that sometimes we may be afraid to try new things; in this case, the children should be encouraged to use Trying When It's Hard (Skill 11) after first using one of the choices listed in this skill.

Read the story *Bootsie Barker Bites,* by Barbara Bottner (Putnam, 1997). Discuss what the girl in the story did to overcome her fear of being bullied.

Read the story *Mirette on the High Wire,* by Emily Arnold McCully (Putnam, 1997). Discuss how each character in the story felt and how Mirette helped Bellini to overcome his fear.

Skill 25: Deciding How Someone Feels

STEPS

1. Watch the person.

Discuss a variety of feelings, such as frustration, anger, happiness, fear, and so on. Help children describe the kinds of body language and words that correspond to these feelings.

2. Name the feeling.

3. Ask.

Decide whether to ask the person if he or she is feeling this way or whether to do something to help that person. If the person seems very angry or upset, point out that it may be best to wait until the person is calm.

SUGGESTED SITUATIONS

School: A large jar of paint was spilled on a child, and he has started to cry.

Home: A parent has dropped a sack of groceries, and he is shaking his head and sighing.

Peer group: A friend of yours asked someone to play, but the person said no.

COMMENTS

This skill extends Reading Others (Skill 14) to include the verbal expression of feelings. Children might also be encouraged to use Offering Help (Skill 18) following this skill if the circumstances warrant.

RELATED SKILL-SUPPORTING ACTIVITY

When reading stories to the children, ask how they think the characters in the story feel and why.

Skill 26: Showing Affection

STEPS

1. Decide if you have nice feelings.

Discuss how to decide if you have positive feelings about someone. Talk about the people children might want to show affection toward (friends, parents, and teachers versus strangers).

2. Choose.

a. Say it.

Talk about things the children might say to friends, parents, or teachers. Guide the children in appropriate things to say.

b. Hug.

Discuss that in many situations it would be appropriate to ask if it's OK to give the person a hug (e.g., a new friend, a teacher).

c. Do something.

Discuss nice things that could be done for someone to show caring.

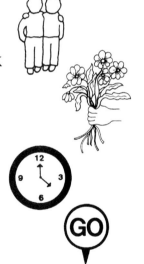

3. When?

Talk about appropriate times to show affection.

4. Do it.

Children should make one of these choices.

SUGGESTED SITUATIONS

School: You want to show your teacher that you like her.

Home: You want to show affection to your grandparents.

Peer group: You want to let a friend know that you like him.

COMMENTS

Because several choices are included in this skill, it may be a difficult one for some younger preschoolers. If so, limit the choices. Some children will need additional help to distinguish between people they know well and comparative strangers. Greeting Others (Skill 13) can be suggested for use with people they know less well.

RELATED SKILL-SUPPORTING ACTIVITY

Display the following headings on the chalkboard or easel pad: "Strangers," "New Friends," "Good Friends." Ask the children for examples of each type (e.g., a store clerk, a sister's friend, your best friend). Write the examples under their respective categories. Ask students whether or not they would show affection to this person and, if so, how.

Skill 27: Dealing with Teasing

STEPS

1. Stop and think.

Discuss the importance of giving yourself time before reacting and the likely consequences of saying something back or acting aggressively. Talk about the reasons people tease (to get others mad or to get their attention).

2. Say, "Please stop."

Stress the importance of Using Brave Talk (Skill 3), and practice this skill.

3. Walk away.

This step is important to help end the teasing situation. After walking away, the child may need to use other skills, such as Asking to Talk (Skill 23) or Relaxing (Skill 32).

SUGGESTED SITUATIONS

School: On the playground, someone is calling you a name.

Home: A brother or sister tells you something that you know isn't true—for example, that your face is blue or that you're going out to dinner when you know you're not.

Peer group: A friend is teasing you that she can ride a bike better than you can.

COMMENTS

It may be important for the young child to talk with another friend or adult about the teasing. If the manner in which the child is talking appears to be "tattling," it is valuable for the child to be guided in Asking to Talk (Skill 23). To ensure safe school environments, it is critical that the student's concern be addressed. Teachers should assess the severity and frequency of the teasing; if the child's responses do not stop the teasing, teacher intervention with the teaser is indicated.

Read and discuss the story *The Cow That Went Oink,* by Bernard Most (Harcourt Brace, 1990).

Make a paper chain with the names of students who have used the skill. Add a link whenever a student reports that he or she has used the skill.

Skill 28: Dealing with Feeling Mad

STEPS

1. Stop and think.

Discuss the importance of stopping and not doing anything. Talk about the negative consequences of acting out this feeling in an aggressive way (e.g., hitting the person). Also discuss that stopping and thinking give a person time to make choices.

2. Choose.

a. Turtle.

Instruct children to act like turtles, curling up in their shells where they can't see the person with whom they are angry.

b. Relax.

Refer to Relaxing (Skill 32).

c. Ask to talk.

Discuss people children can talk to. Refer to Asking to Talk (Skill 23) as needed.

3. Do it.

Children should make one of these choices.

SUGGESTED SITUATIONS

School: The teacher won't let you have free play.

Home: It's raining, and a parent won't let you ride your bike.

Peer group: A friend has taken your basketball and won't give it back.

It is important to offer children a choice involving a physical response, such as relaxing or doing the turtle. The turtle technique is taken from Schneider and Robin's (1974) *Turtle Manual*.

RELATED SKILL-SUPPORTING ACTIVITY

Read the story and do the activities included in the *Turtle Manual*.

Skill 29: Deciding If It's Fair

STEPS

1. **Think about how the other person feels.**
   Discuss thinking about how the other person might feel in a situation that isn't fair (e.g., if the teacher always seems to choose one child to help). Talk about how children feel when they perceive things that aren't fair.

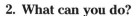

2. **What can you do?**
   Decide if there is anything that could be done to make the situation more fair (e.g., sharing).

3. **Do it.**

SUGGESTED SITUATIONS

School: You or another child has asked the teacher to play with the scooter that someone else is using.

Home: Both you and your brother or sister want to watch different programs on TV, and your parent says you can watch your program.

Peer group: You want to let another friend play, but the child you're playing with doesn't want the other friend to play, too.

COMMENTS

It is very important that the children begin to understand that things can't always be fair. For example, it might rain when you'd planned to go swimming, or you might get the flu and have to stay home from the school skating party.

Present children with several situations (use situations you have observed in the classroom). Give each child a "Fair" and "Not Fair" card. Ask the children to indicate, by holding up the appropriate card, if the situation is fair or not fair. For more information about evaluating situations in terms of fairness, see Camp and Bash's (1981, 1985) Think Aloud program.

Skill 30: Solving a Problem

STEPS

1. **Decide on the problem.**
   Children may need help in defining the problem.

2. **Think of choices.**
   Generate different alternatives children could choose, and discuss the likely consequences of each choice.

3. **Make a plan.**
   Decide on one choice to try and plan how to do this.

4. **Do it.**

SUGGESTED SITUATIONS

School: You have trouble following the teacher's directions.

Home: You have a problem going to bed on time.

Peer group: You like playing with one friend but get upset when another friend comes over to play, too.

COMMENTS

Generating alternatives and anticipating consequences are necessary skills for students to learn. Alternative and consequential thinking, along with goal setting and communication skills, enhance children's social competence (Kupersmidt, 1983).

RELATED SKILL-SUPPORTING ACTIVITY

Have children generate a plan for solving a real-life problem and draw a picture of the plan to share with parents and serve as a reminder to themselves.

Skill 31: Accepting Consequences

STEPS

1. Stop and think.

Stress that this step will give children time to calm down and follow the rest of the steps.

2. Decide if you're wrong.

Discuss that it's OK for people to be wrong. Everyone makes mistakes sometimes.

3. Say, "Yes, I did it. I'm sorry."

Emphasize the importance of Using Nice Talk (Skill 2) when apologizing and being honest when admitting to doing something wrong.

4. Follow the direction.

Explain that children may need to do something to resolve the problem (e.g., clean up a mess or help pay for something they broke).

SUGGESTED SITUATIONS

School: You spilled another child's glass of juice.

Home: You broke something of your parents'.

Peer group: You took a friend's toy without permission.

COMMENTS

Some children may have difficulty verbally admitting their behavior or saying they are sorry. If so, this step could be deleted or another step (perhaps nodding your head yes) could be substituted.

Read *The Tale of Peter Rabbit,* by Beatrix Potter (Warner, 1976). Discuss the mistakes Peter made and how he accepted the consequences.

List common mistakes made by children of this age. Use a puppet or present a picture of an unknown child. As a group, discuss the probable consequences and decide how the puppet or child might respond.

Skill 32: Relaxing

STEPS

1. **Think about how you feel.**
   Talk about how children feel
   when they are tense (jittery
   inside, getting a stomachache,
   tight or warm all over, etc.).

2. **Take three deep breaths.**
   Teach the children how to take relaxing
   breaths: Take a big breath in slowly, then
   let the air out through an open mouth.
   Have everyone practice this step.

3. **Squeeze the oranges.**
   Pretend to give each child an orange in
   each hand. Have children tighten their
   fists to squeeze all the juice out of each
   orange in turn, then both oranges
   together. Finally, have them drop the
   oranges and shake the rest of the juice off
   their hands.

SUGGESTED SITUATIONS

School: You are putting on an important puppet show for another
class.

Home: You are going on vacation, and you're excited; a parent
seems angry with you, and you don't know why.

Peer group: You are waiting to go to a friend's birthday party.

COMMENTS

Children may need a great deal of training in relaxation before
they will be able to use this skill effectively. Having them practice
this skill each day before rest time may help them to fall asleep
more easily.

Practice this skill as a group before a change in routine (e.g., field trips, assemblies) and before classroom activities that are typically difficult for the children.

Skill 33: Dealing with Mistakes

STEPS

1. **Say, "It's OK to make mistakes. Everybody makes mistakes."**
   Discuss mistakes that you have made. Encourage the children to talk about mistakes they have made. Use humor, if appropriate.

2. **Plan for next time.**
   Have children plan how they could avoid making the same mistakes again. Ideas might include taking more time, asking for help, asking a question, and so on.

SUGGESTED SITUATIONS

School: You make a mistake on an art project.

Home: You make a mistake while helping your parent with cooking.

Peer group: You invited a friend over but forgot to ask your parent's permission.

COMMENTS

Discuss how making a plan before engaging in a difficult task may help prevent mistakes, and encourage each child to make such a plan. Because the skill does not require the child to take immediate action, it will be helpful to post the plan in the classroom or at home so the child will have easy reference to it when needed. (Use pictures to illustrate plans for prereaders.)

RELATED SKILL-SUPPORTING ACTIVITY

Have everyone who wants to (including yourself) share "most embarrassing moments."

Skill 34: Being Honest

STEPS

1. Think of what can happen.

Help children construct lists of likely consequences of telling and not telling the
truth. Also discuss how being honest can
sometimes be hurtful (e.g., saying you
don't like a person's haircut).

2. Decide to tell the truth.

Discuss how punishing consequences are
usually less severe if a person is honest
at the start.

3. Say it.

Discuss and practice examples of telling
the truth, such as "I'm sorry I did it" or
"Yes, but I didn't mean to." Emphasize
Using Nice Talk (Skill 2).

SUGGESTED SITUATIONS

School: You accidentally broke one of the school's toys.

Home: You hit your brother or sister when you were angry; you
went across the street without permission.

Peer group: You said something about a friend that was true but
not very nice.

COMMENTS

Children should be rewarded for telling the truth, even though
there may be other negative consequences for their actions.
Encourage children to use Rewarding Yourself (Skill 5) for being
honest.

Spend time discussing the difference between telling "tall tales" and being dishonest. Read the story of Paul Bunyan, and explain that this is a tall tale. Have the children make up their own tall tales. Later, if a child's honesty is questionable, it's OK to ask if he or she is telling a tall tale.

Skill 35: Knowing When to Tell

STEPS

1. Decide if someone will get hurt.

Explain that children need to decide if the action is likely to hurt the person involved, themselves, or someone else.

2. Whom should you tell?

If the action will not result in someone's getting hurt (e.g., one child's taking a toy from another), the child should first talk to the person with whom he or she has the problem, perhaps using Asking a Favor (Skill 7) or Dealing with Teasing (Skill 27) as needed. If the action will cause harm, the child should tell a teacher, parent, or other responsible adult immediately.

3. Do it.

This should be done in a helpful, friendly way.

SUGGESTED SITUATIONS

School: Someone threatens to hit you; someone takes your crayons without asking.

Home: A brother or sister is playing with matches.

Peer group: A friend won't share her candy with you.

COMMENTS

This skill is designed to help children know when to involve an adult in a problem and when to attempt to deal with the problem themselves. Toward this end, discuss different types of things that cause hurt to others, such as hitting, pinching, inappropriate touching, or excessive tickling.

Even when no actual harm will be done, children should feel free to approach adults to discuss ways of dealing with a problem or to talk about the feelings associated with a situation. These are positive behaviors, as opposed to tattling, which has a negative purpose. If a child does approach you about minor peer conflicts, a helpful response is "How can I help you deal with that?"

RELATED SKILL-SUPPORTING ACTIVITY

Develop a list of common situations, and write these (or display pictures of them) on a chart. As a class, decide if children should tell or try to solve the problem themselves. Relative to each situation, discuss or role-play following through with the decision.

Skill 36: Dealing with Losing

STEPS

1. **Say, "Everybody can't win."**
   Point out the absurdity of having everyone win a game. Affirm that it is normal
   to feel disappointed at not winning; discuss the feelings that children have when
   they don't win.

2. **Say, "Maybe I'll win next time."**
   Children should be encouraged to say
   this in a hopeful, coping manner.

3. **Do something else.**
   Point out that, although it's OK to feel
   disappointed, continuing to think about
   the disappointment may only cause
   children to have a bad time.

SUGGESTED SITUATIONS

School: Your group loses at Duck-Duck-Goose (or another game).

Home: You didn't win when playing a game with a brother, sister, or parent.

Peer group: You came in second in a running race with friends.

COMMENTS

Cooperative games and activities such as those described by
Johnson and Johnson (1975) have been found to teach more positive skills than do competitive activities. When possible, cooperative activities, versus competitive ones, should be included in the
school curriculum.

Create times in the classroom when the children can play board games. Prior to beginning the games, set out Dealing with Losing Skill Cards (one fewer than the number of students playing). Tell students that each student who uses the skill after the game should take a card and bring it to you. Congratulate the students for using the skill.

Skill 37: Wanting to Be First

STEPS

1. **Say, "Everybody can't be first."**
   Discuss how the children feel when they are first and when they aren't first. Talk about how it would be impossible for everyone to be first.

2. **Say, "It's OK not to be first."**

3. **Stay with it.**
   Talk about what children would miss if they quit the activity because they weren't first (e.g., the pleasure of playing a game or being part of an activity).

SUGGESTED SITUATIONS

School: You're not first in line for recess or lunch.

Home: A brother or sister gets to sit in the front seat on the way to the park, but you have to wait until the ride home.

Peer group: A friend gets to be first when playing a game.

COMMENTS

Many teachers of preschool or kindergarten children find it helpful to initiate a "Child of the Week" program, in which one child is chosen to share personal things, such as pictures and special toys, and gets to be the line leader and first at special activities. Other teachers choose children to perform specific classroom duties and to be line leaders on a daily basis. Such activities tend to diminish the frequency of children's distress at not being first.

With the children, make a class plan to help them handle the disappointment of not being first (e.g., one child's telling another child to go first). Have the children practice the plan while putting together a jigsaw puzzle. For example, one child is to say, "You can go first." The other can say, "Thank you." Periodically, direct children to use the class plan.

Skill 38: Saying No

STEPS

1. Decide if you want to do it.

The child needs to decide whether or not he or she wants to do what is being asked. Discuss situations when saying no is appropriate and when it is not.

2. If not, why not?

The child should think about his or her reasons for not wanting to do this (e.g., wanting to do something else or feeling it might cause trouble or unnecessarily hurt someone else's feelings).

3. Say, "No."

Stress the importance of Using Nice Talk (Skill 2) when saying no. Point out that the child might also want to give the reason for saying no.

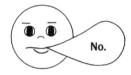

SUGGESTED SITUATIONS

School: A friend wants you to leave the classroom.

Home: A younger brother or sister wants you to stay home and play, but you want to play at a friend's house.

Peer group: A friend wants you to go to the park, but you want to go swimming with another friend.

COMMENTS

Most situations will require Using Nice Talk (Skill 2). However, if a child is being pressured to do something he or she knows is wrong, Using Brave Talk (Skill 3) would be more appropriate.

RELATED SKILL-SUPPORTING ACTIVITY

Read the story *The Toll-Bridge Troll,* by Patricia Rae Wolff (Browndeer, 1995). Discuss how Trigg said no to the troll and whether this was a good way of saying this.

Skill 39: Accepting No

STEPS

1. Stop and think.
Discuss the possible reasons children might be told no in various situations.

2. Choose.

a. Do something else.
Discuss the fact that, even though you are told you can't do or have something, you can still have fun by doing something else.

b. Ask to talk.
Stress that children can use Asking to Talk (Skill 23) if they do not understand the reason for being told no. However, point out that Using Nice Talk (Skill 2) is very important, or the parent or teacher may interpret their questions as arguing. Discuss that the goal of asking is to better understand the adult's decision, not to have the adult change the decision.

3. Do it.
Children should make one of these choices.

SUGGESTED SITUATIONS

School: A teacher tells you that it's time to do art and that you can't have free play.

Home: A parent tells you that it's too late to go to a friend's house to play or that you can't get a toy at the grocery store.

Peer group: A friend tells you that he can't play today or won't let you play with one of his toys.

COMMENTS

This skill may be difficult for many young children to accomplish; many practice sessions should be planned.

RELATED SKILL-SUPPORTING ACTIVITY

Accepting being told no is often very difficult for young children. Develop "Accepting No" cards that depict a special privilege on the back (e.g., computer, book, rocking chair). Throughout the day, when a child uses the skill, let that child choose a card to show which privilege he or she has earned.

Skill 40: Deciding What to Do

STEPS

1. **Think about what you like to do.**
   Help the children generate lists of
   things they like to do that would
   be acceptable in different situations.

2. **Decide on one thing.**

3. **Do it.**

SUGGESTED SITUATIONS

School: It's free play time.

Home: It's a rainy afternoon, and everyone in the house is busy.

Peer group: You and a friend can't think of anything to do.

COMMENTS

After children successfully complete this skill, you may want to
encourage them to use Rewarding Yourself (Skill 5).

RELATED SKILL-SUPPORTING ACTIVITY

Have children draw pictures on index cards of activities they
enjoy. Have each child place his or her cards in a file box under
the headings "Home," "School," and "Outdoors." When a child
complains of not having anything to do, the child can consult his
or her own personal card file.

CHAPTER 7
Refining Skill Use

Although Skillstreaming is derived from social learning theory, cognitive-behavioral interventions such as problem solving, accurate perceptions of social situations, and verbal mediation are embedded in its instructional format and enhance its effectiveness. This chapter examines the role of these approaches in Skillstreaming, as well as that of strategies to increase a child's social performance, including reducing competing problem behaviors, supportive modeling, empathy, and skill shifting/skill combinations.

COGNITIVE-BEHAVIORAL STRATEGIES

Kaplan and Carter (1995) explain the concept of cognition relative to behavioral intervention strategies to include cognitive processes, cognitive structures, and inner speech. *Cognitive processes* involve "more the way we think as opposed to what we think" (p. 381) and can be modified by strategies such as teaching problem solving. *Cognitive structures* relate to our beliefs and ideas. For example, many aggressive youth perceive negative intentions of others, even when actions clearly appear accidental in nature, whereas more socially competent youngsters do not. Finally, *inner speech* is typically referred to as verbal mediation or self-talk. This is the process of using language to guide our thoughts and actions. Incorporating elements of the cognitive-behavioral approach will promote the self-control needed by many young children to change their typical manner of reacting, thus better enabling them to reduce competing problem behavior, recall skill steps, and generalize the skills they learn. Knowledge of the following areas will guide teachers and other group leaders in aspects to include in Skillstreaming instruction that will promote enduring learning and skill use.

Problem Solving

Children may, as Ladd and Mize (1983) point out, be deficient in such problem-solving competencies as identifying the appropriate goal for a social interaction, identifying the desirable behaviors or strategies for reaching a goal, and understanding the context in which specific behaviors are appropriate. Young children may perceive the goal of playing a game with peers as winning instead of having fun, for example. The strategies selected will therefore differ (e.g., cheating to win versus fair play). Cartledge and Feng (1996) state that a purpose of problem-solving instruction is "to teach people how to think through and resolve interpersonal conflicts using a four-step process: (a) identifying and defining the problem, (b) generating a variety of solutions, (c) identifying potential consequences, and (d) implementing and evaluating a solution." Solving a Problem (Skill 30) presents the specific steps for using this process in a social context. However, the cognitive aspect suggests that the general skill of problem solving might be used in conjunction with other skills. Therefore, problem solving may be applied broadly as well as taught as one skill of many. The teacher's challenge, then, is to structure the application of skill use to a variety of situations encountered in children's everyday lives.

Perceptions of Social Situations

Processing social information

Dodge (1983) offers a model for processing social information that is useful in perfecting the skill use of young children. This model includes (a) encoding relevant information, (b) applying meanings, (c) accessing a response, (d) evaluating a response, and (e) enacting a response.

Encoding relevant information. Relative to a social interaction, children must first attend to cues that are appropriate to the interaction. Some children may focus on all of the cues in an interaction, thus having difficulty determining which cues to single out for response. Aggressive children often focus on the cues that appear to them to be aggressive ones. Others may ignore salient social cues—for example, failing to recognize boredom in one's listener when dominating a conversation (Gresham & Elliott, 1990).

Further noted by Gresham and Elliott, "Some children are deficient in a social skill because certain social cues which would prompt socially appropriate behavior are absent" (p. 29). Typical social cues may be absent, for example, when a child is playing with a group of familiar peers.

Applying meanings. One's perception of intent influences one's behavior (Dodge, Murphy, & Birchsbaum, 1984). Meaning is given to the social cue in relation to the individual child's emotional needs or goals. For example, children who often act aggressively may interpret the intent of an action as hostile.

Accessing a response. Children typically do what they know or what is familiar to them. It is far easier for children to access a behavior, and follow through on its performance, when they have mastery of that behavior. Aggressive children, for instance, access more aggressive and less effective ways to solve problems with others (Guerra & Slaby, 1989). The focus of social skills training is to increase these children's repertoire of choices.

Evaluating a response. The capacity to evaluate the potential consequences of an action is associated with social competence. Aggressive youth, for example, identify fewer negative consequences for aggression and view their aggressive choices more positively than do others (Cartledge & Milburn, 1995). In addition, children who are aggressive often believe that their aggression will bring rewards, not negative consequences, including being treated less aversively by others (Perry, Perry, & Rasmussen, 1986).

Enacting a response. The performance of a behavior or skill is relative to the child's proficiency in performing that skill, as well as to his or her motivation to do so.

Social performance, then, involves the enactment of a sequence of behaviors in relevant and appropriate ways within a context. The following sections discuss aspects of social performance to be attended to throughout Skillstreaming instruction.

Social perceptions and behavioral flexibility

Even if a student becomes proficient in a given skill, the student may misread the context in which the prosocial skill is desirable or acceptable. Although the procedures to teach social skills are the same as those in teaching academics, the teaching of social skills is more complex due to the reciprocal nature of social interactions. With academic instruction, it is often the case that there is one, and only one, correct response. Furthermore, that correct response is always correct. Social skills performance, on the other hand, is influenced by culture, setting, and group dynamics (Scott & Nelson, 1998).

A major emphasis in psychology for the past 15 years concerns the importance of the situation or setting, as perceived by the individual, in determining behavior. Morrison and Bellack (1981), for example, state that individuals must not only possess the ability to enact given behavioral skills, they must also know when and how these responses should be applied. These authors further state that in order to use this knowledge, individuals must have the "ability to accurately 'read' the social environment" (p. 70). This ability, they suggest, includes awareness of the norms and conventions in operation at a given time as well as understanding of the message given by the other person. The work of Dil (1972), Emery (1975), and Rothenbert (1970) suggests that emotionally disturbed and "socially maladjusted" youngsters are characteristically deficient in such social perceptiveness.

We believe that students can be taught to read the context (situation and setting) of the social situation accurately and adjust their behavior accordingly. Therefore, emphasis must be placed not only on skill performance, but also on such questions as the following: "What is the behavior expected in this setting?" "Which skill should I use with this person, considering his or her role?" and "What signs are there that this is a good time to use the skill?" Attending to such questions while teaching behavioral skills will likely result in more successful skill use and guide students in developing the flexibility needed to adjust skill use across settings, situations, and people.

The work of Dodge (1985) and Spivack and Shure (1974) suggests that children should be able to respond to the following questions throughout their skill performance:

- Why should I use the skill?

- With whom should I use the skill?

- Where should I use the skill?

- When should I use the skill?

- How should I perform the skill?

Although many of these issues are addressed in the skills themselves as particular behavioral steps and in the four components of Skillstreaming (modeling, role-playing, performance feedback, and generalization), additional emphasis can be achieved via group discussion, supplementary role-play practice, and related activities.

Why should I use the skill? Children will be more likely to learn a new behavior or skill if they are motivated to do so. Understanding how prosocial skill performance will help them meet their needs—get the favor they want or need, stay out of trouble, and so forth—is valuable in enhancing motivation. Therefore, as teachers and other group leaders introduce each skill, they must point out the specific and direct benefits to be gained.

With whom should I use the skill? To perform the skill competently, the child must learn to assess and interpret the verbal and nonverbal cues of the person(s) to whom the skill performance is directed. For example, it is sometimes the case that a child who is learning Joining In (Skill 15) fails to assess the receptivity of the target peer group. If the group appears to be avoiding the skill-deficient child (i.e., continuing to move the activity away, refusing to make eye contact, or even shouting at the child to go away), the child will need to learn how to attend to such cues and interpret their meaning. The teacher can help by guiding the child in selecting another person or group to approach or by urging the child to use a related back-up skill with the first group. Likewise, although Saying No (Skill 38) may help avoid trouble when directed toward a friend, the outcome may be quite different if the skill is tried with a parent who is directing the child to get ready for school. Such parameters of skill use may not be easily identified by many young children, and discussions and perhaps role plays of this issue will need to be an integral part of instruction.

Where should I use the skill? The skill-deficient child will need help in evaluating the setting in which he or she intends to use the skill. A child's using Asking Someone to Play (Skill 19), for instance, may be desirable during classroom free play or during outside recess but would not be desirable while grocery shopping with a parent. Although adults may assume that most children automatically make this type of determination, this has not proven to be the case. Instead, varied settings in which the skill will likely be successful or unsuccessful should be addressed through group discussion and multiple role plays.

When should I use the skill? When a skill should be used is often a question for the preschool or kindergarten child. It is not unusual, for example, for the child to use Asking a Question (Skill 9) while the teacher is giving directions or while a parent is involved in an interaction with another person. Therefore, discussions related to the timing of skill use need to be included with each skill.

How should I perform the skill? The manner in which a child performs a skill can determine its effectiveness. For example, a child who uses Asking a Favor (Skill 7) in an angry manner will likely find that the favor is not granted. Likewise, the child who employs the steps of Dealing with Teasing (Skill 27) but who is obviously upset at being provoked may not find that the skill yields a positive outcome. Two behavioral skills to be taught early on therefore deal solely with the manner in which a skill is delivered: Using Nice Talk (Skill 2), to encourage the child to employ a friendly manner, and Using Brave Talk (Skill 3), to encourage the child to make an assertive response.

Nonverbal Behaviors

Nonverbal communicators such as body posture and movements, facial expressions, and voice tone and volume give others messages either consistent with or contradictory to verbal content. Consider, for example, a child who is told by a playground supervisor to leave the playground for not following the rules. Often it is not the breaking of the rule per se that results in the playground expulsion. When the playground supervisor is further questioned regarding the child's defiance or failure to show remorse, nonverbal evidence may be called upon (e.g., "She acted like it wasn't her fault" or "He didn't look sorry!"). Understanding the influence of nonverbal language is an important factor in learning prosocial behaviors. In brief, skill-deficient students will need to be made more aware of the ways in which nonverbal communicators send clear and definite messages.

Verbal Mediation

Much of the early work on children's use of language to regulate their own behaviors was done by the Russian psychologist Luria (1961). This pattern of language development is described by Little and Kendall (1979) as "The process of development of verbal control of behavior" (p. 101). Verbal mediation, or saying aloud what would normally be said to oneself silently, is a valuable and necessary part of both modeling and role-playing. Saying the steps aloud as the models or role players enact the behaviors demonstrates the cognitive processes underlying skill performance and facilitates learning. For example, when performing the skill of Dealing with Fear (Skill 24), the model might say, "My stomach is upset. It's hard to think. I know I am afraid." The first step is "What?" (What causes me to feel afraid?). This type of accompanying narration increases the effectiveness of the modeling display (Bandura, 1977), draws observers' attention to specific skill steps, and may facilitate skill generalization (Stokes & Baer, 1977). Verbal mediation may also be employed to demonstrate a coping model. For example, "I know I can relax, but it's difficult to do when I feel this way."

Verbal mediation techniques have been used to teach impulse control in hyperactive children (Kendall & Braswell, 1985), anger control in adolescents (Goldstein, Glick, & Gibbs, 1998), impulse control in aggressive youngsters (Camp & Bash, 1981), and academic behaviors through self-instruction training (Meichenbaum, 1977). By practicing talking themselves through a skill or saying aloud ways to control the impulse to react in an undesirable way, students learn to regulate their actions until these actions become nearly automatic. As stated by Camp and Bash (1985):

> A good deal of evidence suggests that adequate development of verbal mediation activity is associated with

(1) internalization of the inhibitory function of language, which serves to block impulsive and associative responding in both cognitive and social situations, and (2) utilization of linguistic tools in learning, problem-solving, and forethought. (p. 7)

Many young children will need to be taught the process of thinking aloud by practicing while they are engaged in other types of activities (e.g., completing academic tasks, doing classroom chores). Activities useful in teaching children the technique of verbal mediation are described at length by Camp and Bash (1981, 1985).

REDUCING COMPETING PROBLEM BEHAVIORS

Many children may know the desired and expected behavior and may, in fact, be likely to behave in this manner in many situations. However, when angry, anxious, or otherwise upset, they are unable to see beyond the emotion-producing event. Before many children will be able to recall the steps of a specific skill, they must use strategies to stop themselves from reacting with a perhaps well-established pattern of aggression or another unproductive behavior. Such impulse control procedures are often referred to as *coping skills* or *self-regulation strategies.*

One such strategy is Feindler's Anger Control Training (Feindler, 1979; Feindler & Ecton, 1986), which facilitates such skill behavior indirectly, by teaching ways to inhibit anger and loss of self-control. In this method, children are taught how to respond to provocations to anger by (a) identifying their external and internal anger triggers; (b) identifying their own physiological/kinesthetic cues signifying anger; (c) using anger reducers to lower arousal via deep breathing, counting backwards, visualizing, or contemplating the long-term consequences of anger-associated behavior; (d) using reminders or self-statements that are in opposition to triggers; and (e) self-evaluating, or judging how adequately anger control worked and rewarding oneself when it has worked well. Although Anger Control Training includes too many steps for the preschool and kindergarten child to master in its entirety, understanding this sequence will help in teaching of impulse control and in prompting the child through the process during real-life situations.

The majority of Skillstreaming skills that are used under stressful conditions include an anger or impulse control strategy—counting to five or taking three deep breaths, for example. Emphasizing these methods, taking additional time to teach them and reinforce their use, or using all or part of the Anger Control Training process just described will increase the likelihood of success in students' real-life skill use.

Gresham (1998) explains that the problematic behavior may be more efficient for the child. In other words, the outcome the child desires is easier to obtain through using the problem behavior than through using an alternative, more socially acceptable behavior or skill. The problem behavior is also likely to be reliable as well, consistently leading to reinforcement for the individual. A goal, then, is to reduce the reliability and efficiency of the problem behavior. Therefore, for children whose emotional responses inhibit or prevent skill performance, Elliott and Gresham (1991) suggest that instruction in the prosocial skill be paired with strategies to reduce the interfering problem behavior.

SUPPORTIVE MODELING

Typically, aggressive children are exposed to highly aggressive models. Peers, parents, and siblings are often chronically aggressive individuals themselves (Knight & West, 1975; Loeber & Dishion, 1983; Robins, West, & Herjanic, 1975). At the same time, relatively few prosocial models that might help counteract the effects of aggressive modeling exist for these youngsters to observe and imitate. When prosocial models are available, they apparently can make a tremendous difference in social development. Werner and Smith (1982), in their longitudinal study of aggressive and nonaggressive youth, titled *Vulnerable but Invincible*, clearly demonstrate that youth growing up in a community characterized by high crime, high unemployment, high secondary school dropout rates, and high levels of aggressive modeling were able to develop into effective, satisfied, prosocially oriented individuals if they had sustained exposure to at least one significant prosocial model—be it parent, relative, teacher, coach, neighbor, or peer.

The classroom teacher can be a powerful model for students. Needless to say, a powerful negative effect can be exerted on students if the teacher models prosocial skill deficiencies. Throughout the course of the school day, the teacher should make a sustained effort to model desirable, prosocial behaviors and to use the behavioral steps for selected skills when it is appropriate to do so. When frustrated or angry with an individual student's behavior, for example, the teacher can greatly affect student learning by modeling the steps of Dealing with Feeling Mad (Skill 28) in a clear and deliberate manner.

EMPATHY

Very young children possess the capacity to show empathy. Denham (1998), citing the work of Zahn-Waxler and Radke-Yarrow (1982, 1990), states that "children as young as two years of age are able to broadly interpret others' emotional states, to experience these feeling states in response to others' predicament, and attempt to alleviate discomfort in others" (p. 34). Chronically aggressive or other skill-deficient youth have been shown to display a pattern of personality traits high in egocentricity and low in concern for others (Slavin, 1980). Expression of empathic understanding can serve both as an inhibitor of negative behaviors and as a facilitator of positive actions. Results of a number of studies inquiring into the interpersonal consequences of empathic responding show that empathy is a consistently potent promoter of interpersonal attraction, dyadic openness, conflict resolution, and individual growth (Goldstein & Michaels, 1985). In other words, children who are able to show empathy are far less likely to act out aggressively toward others, are more accepted and sought after in social situations, are more able to participate in resolving interpersonal disputes, and are more satisfied with themselves.

Some helpful methods of encouraging empathy include (a) instructing children in skills such as Deciding How Someone Feels (Skill 25); (b) providing opportunities for role reversal during role plays, followed by actors' expression of feelings; (c) providing opportunities for observers to take the perspective of others (e.g., that of the main actor) during feedback sessions; and (d) encouraging empathy toward others through the modeling and discussion of appreciation for individual differences.

SKILL SHIFTING/SKILL COMBINATIONS

Skill shifting refers to the selection and performance of an alternative skill when one skill is not successful for the child. Although the training setting is designed to provide for the successful outcome of skill performance, we know that in real life even a highly competent performance may fail to bring about the desired outcome. This failure may be the result of inaccurate assessment of the receptivity of the other individuals involved or of aspects of the setting, such as the degree of structure imposed. Despite the uncontrollability of the world outside the Skillstreaming setting, it is important to reward the child for his or her attempts and, whenever possible, to offer opportunities for repeated practice in making other prosocial skill choices when initial choices fail. Thus, group instruction should help the child discern when a skill is unsuccessful, when an alternative skill should be tried, and which specific skill should be attempted. For example, Sammy attempts the skill of Joining In (Skill 15) on the playground during recess and finds the attempt unsuccessful. He may need to shift to another skill, such as Feeling Left Out (Skill 22) or Deciding What to Do (Skill 40). When such lack of success in using a skill seems to permeate the child's attempts in real life, a combination of skills should be taught. In the previous example, if using the skill of Joining In consistently fails to bring about a desired response, Sammy will likely need to use a skill combination (e.g., Joining In and Deciding What to Do) to find satisfaction in both attempting the skill and enjoying himself during recess.

SUMMARY

Incorporating cognitive-behavioral strategies will enhance the effectiveness of Skillstreaming instruction. This chapter has addressed strategies that are embedded within specific skills and the instructional presentation, such as problem solving, perceptions of social situations, and verbal mediation. Social competence, as discussed in this chapter, extends beyond the performance of isolated skills. Additional techniques to enhance the child's performance of the Skillstreaming curriculum, in addition to enhancing the potential success of skill use, have been discussed.

CHAPTER 8

Teaching for Skill Generalization

As the social skills movement in general and Skillstreaming in particular have matured, and evidence regarding Skillstreaming's effectiveness has accumulated, it has become clear that skill acquisition is a reliable finding across both training methods and populations. However, generalization is another matter. Both generalization to new settings (transfer) and over time (maintenance) have been reported in only a minority of cases. The main concern of any teaching effort is not how students perform in the teaching setting, but how well they perform in their real lives. This chapter examines approaches to enhance skill generalization. These procedures, which collectively constitute the current technology of transfer and maintenance enhancement, are listed in Table 3 and examined in detail in the following pages.

GENERALIZATION CONCERNS

Many traditional interventions have reflected a core belief in personality change as both the target and outcome of effective intervention; thus environmental influences on behavior have been largely ignored. It has been assumed that the positive changes believed to have taken place within the individual's personality would enable the individual to deal effectively with problematic events wherever and whenever they might occur. That is, transfer and maintenance would occur automatically.

Research on psychotherapy, initiated in the 1950s and expanded in the 1960s and 1970s, sought to ascertain whether gains at the end of the formal intervention had generalized across

---

TABLE 3   **Transfer- and Maintenance-Enhancing Procedures**

Transfer	Maintenance
1. Provision of general principles (general case programming)	*During the Skillstreaming session*
2. Overlearning (maximizing response availability)	1. Thinning reinforcement (increase intermittency, unpredictability)
3. Stimulus variability (training sufficient exemplars, training loosely)	2. Delaying reinforcement
	3. Fading prompts
4. Identical elements (programming common stimuli)	4. Providing booster sessions
	5. Preparing for real-life nonreinforcement
5. Mediated generalization (self-reinforcement, self-monitoring)	*Beyond the Skillstreaming session*
	6. Programming for reinforcement in the natural environment
6. Reduction of competing behaviors	7. Using natural reinforcers

---

settings and/or time. Stokes and Baer (1977) described this time as one in which transfer and maintenance were hoped for and noted if they did occur ("train and hope").

The overwhelming result of these investigations was that, much more often than not, transfer and maintenance of intervention gains did not occur. Treatment and training did not persist automatically, nor did learning necessarily transfer (Goldstein & Kanfer, 1979; Keeley, Shemberg, & Carbonell, 1976). This failure, as revealed by evidence accumulated during the train-and-hope phase, led to a third phase—the energetic development, evaluation, and use of procedures explicitly designed to enhance transfer and maintenance of intervention gains.

TRANSFER-ENHANCING PROCEDURES

The effort to develop a way to maximize transfer and maintenance has resulted in considerable success. A variety of useful techniques have been developed, evaluated, and incorporated in practice.

Provision of General Principles

Transfer of training may be facilitated by providing the child with the general mediating principles that govern satisfactory performance on both the original and the transfer task. The child can be given the rules, strategies, or organizing principles that lead to successful performance. The general finding that understanding the principles underlying successful performance can enhance transfer to new tasks and contexts has been reported in a number of domains of psychological research, including studies of labeling, rules, advance organizers, and learning sets. It is a robust finding, with empirical support in both laboratory and psychoeducational settings.

No matter how competently Skillstreaming leaders seek to create in the role-play setting the "feel" of the real-life setting in which the student will need to use the skill, and no matter how well the coactor in a given role play matches the actual qualities the real target person possesses, there will always be differences between role play and real world. Even when the child has role-played the skill a number of times, the demands of the actual situation will depart at least in some respects from the demands portrayed in the role play. And the real parent, real peer, or real teacher is likely to respond at least somewhat differently than did the child's role-play partner. When the child has a good grasp of the principles underlying a situation (demands, expected behaviors, norms, purposes, rules) and the principles underlying the skill (why these steps, in this order, toward which ends), successful transfer of skilled performance becomes more likely.

Overlearning

Transfer of training has been shown to be enhanced by procedures that maximize overlearning or response availability: The likelihood that a response will be available is clearly a function of its prior use. We repeat and repeat foreign language phrases we are trying to learn, we insist that our child spend an hour per day in piano practice, and we devote considerable time practicing to make a golf swing smooth and "automatic." These are simply expressions of the response-availability notion—that is, the more we have practiced responses (especially correct ones), the easier it will be to use them in other contexts or at later times. We need not rely solely on everyday experience to find support for this conclusion. It has been well established empirically that, other things being equal, the response emitted most frequently in the past is more likely to be emitted on subsequent occasions. However, it is not sheer practice of attempts at effective behaviors that is of most benefit to transfer, but practice of *successful* attempts. Overlearning involves extending learning over more trials than would be necessary merely to produce initial changes in the individual's behavior. In all too many instances of teaching, one or two successes at a given task are taken as evidence to move on to the next task or the next level of the original task. This is an error if one wishes to maximize transfer via overlearning. To maximize transfer, the guiding rule should not be "practice makes perfect" (implying that one simply practices until one gets it right and then moves on), but "practice of perfect" (implying numerous overlearning trials of correct responses after the initial success).

Some children who have just received good feedback from group members and leaders about their role play (all steps followed and well portrayed) may object to the request that they role-play the skill a second or third time. Although valid concerns exist about the consequences of boredom when teaching a group of potentially restless children, the value of skill repetition cannot be overstressed. Often leaders, not children, are most bothered or bored by the repetition. To assuage any student concerns, leaders can point to the value for professional athletes of warm-ups, shoot-arounds, batting practice, and other repetitive practice. Such practice makes core skills nearly automatic and frees the player to concentrate on strategy.

In many real-life contexts, people and events actually work against the child's use of prosocial behaviors. It is therefore quite common and appropriate for a Skillstreaming group to spend two, three, or even more sessions role-playing a single skill. To reduce the possible interference of new learning on previously learned materials, a second skill should be introduced only when the child can recall the steps of the first skill, has had opportunities to role-play it, and has shown some initial transfer outside of the group teaching setting (e.g., a successfully completed homework assignment).

Stimulus Variability

In the previous section, we addressed enhancement of transfer by means of practice and repetition—that is, by the sheer number of correct skill responses the child makes in a given situation. Transfer is also enhanced by the variability or range of situations to which the individual responds. Teaching related to even two situations is better than teaching related to one. As noted several years ago, "The implication is clear that in order to maximize positive transfer, training should provide for some sampling of the population of stimuli to which the response must ultimately be given" (Goldstein, Heller, & Sechrest, 1966, p. 220). As Kazdin (1975) comments:

> One way to program response maintenance and transfer
> of training is to develop the target behavior in a variety of
> situations and in the presence of several individuals. If
> the response is associated with a range of settings, indi-
> viduals, and other cues, it is less likely to be lost when
> the situations change. (p. 21)

Epps, Thompson, and Lane (1985) discuss stimulus variability for transfer enhancement as it might operate in school contexts under the rubrics "train sufficient examples" and "train loosely." They observe that generalization of new skills or behaviors can also be facilitated by training students under a wide variety of conditions. Manipulating the number of leaders, settings, and response classes involved in the intervention promotes generalization by exposing students to a variety of situations. If, for purposes of overlearning, students are asked to role-play a given skill correctly, let us say, three times, each attempt should involve a different coactor, a different setting, and, especially, a different need for the same skill.

Identical Elements

In perhaps the earliest experimental work dealing with transfer enhancement, Thorndike and Woodworth (1901) concluded that, when one habit had a facilitative effect on another, it was to the degree that the habits shared identical elements. Ellis (1965) and Osgood (1953) later emphasized the importance for transfer of similarity between characteristics of the training and application tasks. As Osgood (1953) noted: "The greater the similarity between practice and test stimuli, the greater the amount of positive transfer" (p. 213). This conclusion rests on solid experimental support.

In Skillstreaming, the principle of identical elements is implemented by procedures that increase the "real-lifeness" of the stimuli (places, people, events, etc.) to which the leader is helping the child learn to respond with effective, satisfying behaviors. Two broad strategies exist for attaining such high levels of correspondence between in-group and extra-group stimuli. The first concerns the location in which Skillstreaming takes place. Typically, we remain in the school or institution and by use of props and imagination try to recreate the feel of the real-world context in which the child plans to use the skill. Whenever possible, however, the Skillstreaming group leaves the formal teaching setting and meets in the actual locations in which the problem behaviors occur: "Fight on the playground? Let's have our session there." "Playing alone during free play in the gym? Let's move there." "Argument with a peer in the recess line? Today's group will meet in the hallway."

In addition to implementing identical elements by using real-world locations, Skillstreaming employs the principle of transfer enhancement by having co-trainees in the group be the same people the child interacts with on a regular basis outside of the group. It is especially valuable to employ such a strategy when the others involved are persons the child is not getting along with well and with whom more prosocially skilled interactions are desired. Suppose, for example, you are starting two Skillstreaming groups of eight children each. Two of the children fight a lot. For most interventions, for the sake of behavior management, one child would be placed in one group, the second in the other. Not so in Skillstreaming. If children fight, put them in the same group and hope that conflict occurs during a group session. These two children are real-world figures for each other. They employ poor quality prosocial behaviors in their chronic inability to get along outside the group. What a fine opportunity their participation in the same group presents to teach them positive alternatives for dealing with their real-life difficulties.

Thus if given the choice in starting a single Skillstreaming group, we would select all of its members from one class or unit, rather than one or a few each from more than one group. Live together, play together, go to class together, fight or argue together—you learn Skillstreaming together. For the same reason, when implementing Skillstreaming in residential, agency, or institutional settings, our teaching groups are most often constructed to parallel the facility's unit, crew, cottage, or ward structure.

Mediated Generalization

The one certain commonality, by definition present in both teaching and application settings, is the target child. Mediated generalization—mediated by the child, not by others—is an approach to transfer enhancement that relies on instructing the individual in a series of context-bridging, self-regulation competencies (Neilans & Israel, 1981). Operationally, it consists of instructing the child in self-recording (self-monitoring), self-reinforcement, self-punishment, and self-instruction. Two of these mediation strategies—self-reinforcement and self-monitoring—are particularly useful for the preschool and kindergarten child.

Self-reinforcement

Often, environmental support is insufficient to maintain newly learned skills. In fact, as mentioned earlier, many real-life environments actually discourage children's efforts to behave prosocially. For this reason, we have found it useful to include the teaching of self-reinforcement and self-monitoring procedures. Many young children are far more motivated to use newly learned skills when they, rather than an outside observer, monitor and report or record their use of a skill.

The child's continued use of a learned skill should be encouraged by ongoing reinforcement and monitoring of skill use. Self-monitoring provides a reinforcing function in itself. This may consist of the child's verbally reporting skill use and may include self-recording. For example, if the student follows all the steps of a particular skill especially well, self-reinforcement might take the form of saying something positive (e.g., "Good for me" or "I did a good job"). Teachers can help encourage the child by having him or her rehearse self-rewarding statements following completion of homework assignments or after spontaneous skill use.

Self-monitoring

Self-monitoring involves the child's noting when a skill has been performed and documenting his or her own skill performance. For example, the child may place a sticker or star on a card, or color a space or happy face, when he or she performs the skill. The sample self-monitoring form (shown in Figure 8) is associated with one such plan. In using this form, the teacher identifies the skill for practice, and the child colors a spot on the giraffe each time the skill is performed. When all the spots have been colored, the child is allowed to keep the picture of the giraffe as a reinforcer. A stronger reinforcer (e.g., an additional tangible reward or special privilege) may be provided, particularly if the child has been successful in achieving repeated skill performance to remediate a particularly problematic behavior. This type of plan lends itself best to skills that can be performed in view of the teacher, especially for preschoolers, who may not accurately report their own behavior. Examples of other self-monitoring forms are included in the Program Forms book or may be created as needed.

Reduction of Competing Behaviors

Generalization failure may also be related to competing behaviors—those behaviors that the child knows well and that seem to work (i.e., achieve the outcome desired). To further explain this concept, Gresham (1998) states: "One reason, among many, that socially skilled behaviors may fail to generalize is because the newly taught behavior is masked or overpowered by older and stronger competing behaviors" (p. 23). Competing behaviors often interfere because they may be more efficient (the reinforcer is easier to obtain) and more reliable (consistently lead to reinforcement) than the newly learned prosocial behavior or skill. Such interference helps to explain why some behaviors or skills fail to generalize and why some behaviors, once learned and maintained, deteriorate over time (Gresham, 1998). Therefore, interventions

FIGURE 8 Self-Monitoring Form: Example 2

I reached
my goal!

Name _____ Elizabeth _____
Date _____ 10/15/02 _____
Skill _____ Asking for Help (#6) _____

designed to reduce competing behaviors, such as applying logical consequences or other behavior change strategies, may need to be implemented to facilitate generalization of desirable skills.

MAINTENANCE-ENHANCING PROCEDURES

The persistence, durability, or maintenance of behaviors developed by skills training approaches is primarily a matter of the manipulation of reinforcement both during the original teaching and in the child's natural environment. There are several ways of manipulating such maintenance-enhancing reinforcement. We will first examine what can be done during the Skillstreaming session, then turn to ways to increase generalization beyond the Skillstreaming group.

During the Skillstreaming Session

Thinning reinforcement

A rich, continuous reinforcement schedule is optimal for the establishment of new behaviors. Maintenance of learned behaviors will be enhanced if the reinforcement schedule is gradually thinned. Thinning of reinforcement proceeds best by moving from a continuous (every trial) schedule, to some form of intermittent schedule, to the level of sparse and infrequent reinforcement characteristic of the natural environment. In fact, the goal of such a thinning process is to make the reinforcement schedule indistinguishable from that typically found in real-world contexts. For example, the child will initially receive a reward for each time the skill is used (e.g., Homework 1 Report), then the reinforcement will gradually be thinned and the child will receive the reward (perhaps a larger or more desirable reward) for two or more skill performances (e.g., Homework 2 Report).

Delaying reinforcement

Resistance to extinction is also enhanced by delaying reinforcement. During the early stages of learning a new skill, immediate reinforcement contingent upon display of that behavior or skill is necessary. Once the skill has become a part of the child's behavioral repertoire, reinforcement should be delayed, more closely approximating the reinforcing conditions in the natural environment (Epps et al., 1985).

Delay of reinforcement may be implemented, according to Sulzer-Azaroff and Mayer (1991), by (a) increasing the size or complexity of the responses required before reinforcement is provided; (b) adding a time delay between the response and the delivery of reinforcement; and (c) in token systems, increasing the interval between the receipt of tokens and the opportunity to spend them and/or requiring more tokens in exchange for a given reinforcer. For example, the child may initially be rewarded for performing the skill in his or her real life (e.g., choose from the prize box), then the child may instead receive a token or ticket for each performance. When a given number of tickets are earned, the child may exchange these for a reward (e.g., make a choice from a box with bigger prizes) or a special privilege at the end of the day (e.g., free play). Later on, an increased number of tickets may be required to earn an even larger reward (e.g., lunch with the teacher).

Fading prompts

Prompting may involve describing the specific types of situations in the real world in which students should use a given skill (i.e., instructed generalization; Stokes & Baer, 1977). Children can be encouraged to use a particular skill, or verbally prompted, in a variety of real-life settings. Historically, teachers have used this principle of generalization by prompting students during "teachable moments," or times the skill is actually needed. When potential problems arise in the classroom, the teacher can elicit a prosocial response by suggesting a particular skill. For example, Todd, who often became disruptive in the classroom, had completed his workbook page and was sitting quietly at his desk; rather than waiting for Todd to become disruptive, the teacher suggested that he use Deciding What to Do (Skill 40). This proactive approach turns naturally occurring problem situations into realistic learning opportunities, thus providing more opportunities for practice. Furthermore, it helps create a positive environment for learning ways to deal with interpersonal problems.

Another way of prompting skill use is to provide written prompts in the form of Skill Cards (teacher made or the preprinted variety available from Research Press) or teacher-made skill posters. Cue cards may also be teacher-developed, listing the skill's behavioral steps and including spaces for the child to check off each step, either as the step is enacted or after all steps are completed. The child may tape a card of this type to the table area where he or she works, if it is a skill that is to be used in the classroom, or keep it in a pocket or folder, if it is for use in another setting (e.g., on the school bus, on the playground, at home). For example, Ayul needed to practice Joining In (Skill 15) on the playground. The cue card Ayul's teacher made for her is shown in Figure 9.

Displaying a poster of a given skill will help children remember to practice it. Placed wherever it is most appropriate, the skill poster gives the name of the skill and lists and illustrates its behavioral steps. If the children have been instructed in the skills of Asking Someone to Play (Skill 19) and Playing a Game (Skill 20), for example, displaying posters for these skills in the area of the classroom used for free play may remind the children of these particular skills and skill steps.

Maintenance may be enhanced by the gradual removal of such suggestions, reminders, coaching, or instruction. Fading of prompts is a means of moving away from artificial control (the teacher's) to more natural self-control of desirable behaviors. As is true for all the enhancement techniques examined here, fading of prompts should be carefully planned and systematically implemented.

Providing booster sessions

Periodically, it may be necessary to reinstate instruction in order for certain prosocial behaviors to continue in the natural environment. Booster sessions between teacher and student, either on a preplanned schedule or as needed, have often proven valuable in this regard (Feindler & Ecton, 1986; Karoly & Steffen, 1980). When the teacher, for instance, notices that skills previously taught are not used on a consistent basis, these sessions may also be carried out with the group as a whole. In such cases, the skill is retaught via the same methods as initially presented (modeling, role-playing, performance feedback, and generalization). Because the instruction is a review of the skill, the session will likely move more quickly than initial skill instruction.

FIGURE 9 Ayul's Cue Card

Joining In

1. Move closer.

2. Watch.

3. Ask.

 I did it!

Preparing for real-life nonreinforcement

Both teacher and child may take energetic steps to maximize the likelihood that reinforcement for appropriate behaviors will occur in the natural environment. Nevertheless, on a number of occasions, reinforcement will not be forthcoming. Thus it is important for the child to be prepared for this eventuality. As described previously in this chapter, self-reinforcement is one option when desirable behaviors are performed correctly but are unrewarded by external sources.

Graduated homework assignments. The student may also be prepared for nonreinforcement in the natural environment by completing graduated homework assignments. It may become clear as Skillstreaming homework is discussed that the real-life figure is too difficult a target, too harsh, too unresponsive, or simply too unlikely to provide reinforcement for competent skill use. When this is the case, with the newly learned skill still fragile, we have redirected the homework assignment toward two or three more benevolent target figures. When the child finally does use the skill correctly with the original target figure and receives no reinforcement, his or her previously reinforced trials help minimize the likelihood that the behavior will be extinguished.

Group reward plan. In this procedure, the teacher (or the children included in the skills group or class) decides on a target skill. Most often, this skill will be one recently taught in the Skillstreaming group or one that the children need an extra reminder to use throughout the day. Each time any child (or even the teacher) performs the skill, a block is colored on the Group Reward Form (for a sample, see Figure 5, on page 68). When all of the blocks have been colored, the entire group earns a special reward, such as a popcorn party, an extra recess period, or a favorite story. Other types of group plans similar to this example may be created by the teacher. Using a plan in which all group members work together to achieve a common goal helps to create a cooperative spirit in the classroom and will often result in children's reminding one another to use the skill when a situation suggests its use.

Skill tickets. To encourage the continued use of prosocial skills in the preschool or kindergarten setting, token reinforcers such as the Skill Ticket shown in Figure 6 (on page 69) may be given throughout the school day when individual children use any prosocial skill. The tickets can be accumulated until a given number are earned, then redeemed for a special activity or reward. If necessary, these tickets may also be given in the Skillstreaming group itself to encourage following group rules, role-playing, and completing homework assignments. Such tokens should always be paired with verbal praise. It is also important that each child's name appear on these tickets and that a special place be provided in which to store them.

Skill notes. Teachers typically send notes home to parents pertaining to preacademic or behavioral achievements. Skill Notes such as the one illustrated in Figure 7 (on page 69) can be completed and sent home with a child who has demonstrated skill use in the classroom or in another school environment. If the child is unlikely to get the note home or receive praise at home for skill use, it will be important that he or she take the note to another person in the school setting (e.g., principal, librarian, other teacher) before taking the note home. Again, the purpose of such notes is to provide the child with additional reinforcement for prosocial skill use and to communicate to others which specific skills are being emphasized at school.

Awards. Children are more likely to continue their attempts to use a prosocial skill if they are rewarded by significant others in their environment. Awards may be given by the teacher, principal, and/or parents.

The Teacher Award is a type of material reinforcer to be given after children have attained proficiency in some or all of the skills included in one of the six main skill groups. Figure 10 illustrates an award given for achievement in Group IV (Dealing with Feelings). These awards may be displayed in the classroom on a bulletin board reserved for this purpose and then taken home by the child to show to parents.

Whenever a teacher or another person in the school environment observes a child using a prosocial skill, the child may be sent to the principal's or director's office to receive a Principal Award, along with words of praise and encouragement (for a sample, see Figure 11). Such reinforcement from a person in authority may provide a strong reinforcer to the child to continue to use prosocial behaviors.

The Parent Award, illustrated in Figure 12, is designed to be used by parents who have been involved in a Skillstreaming training session and who will likely notice prosocial skill use in the home setting. The Parent Award identifies the prosocial skill parents should watch for and includes a space so parents can sign the award and return it to school with the child once the skill is observed. The awards can then be displayed in the classroom as appropriate. This method provides additional reinforcement to the child as he or she attempts skill use outside of the classroom.

Goal setting. Setting individual goals is a form of self-management that can have a powerful effect on learning. The preschool or kindergarten child has the capacity to participate in identifying a specific social goal toward which to direct learning efforts. In many classrooms, individual social goals are posted in

FIGURE 10   Teacher Award

Dealing with Feelings Award

Name _____ Sammy _____
Date _____ 10/15/02 _____

FIGURE 11   **Principal Award**

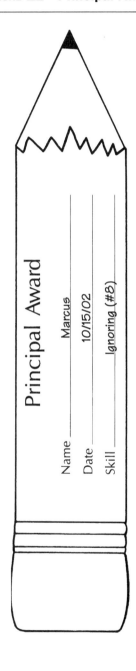

Principal Award

Name _____ Marcus _____
Date _____ 10/15/02 _____
Skill _____ Ignoring (#8) _____

FIGURE 12   **Parent Award**

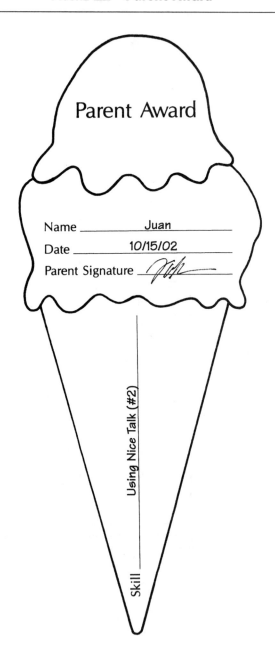

Parent Award

Name _____ Juan _____

Date _____ 10/15/02 _____

Parent Signature _____

Skill ___ Using Nice Talk (#2)

the child's work area. Figure 13 shows a teacher-made goal-setting card that might be used in this way. In other classrooms, skill steps are written on a blank nametag and worn by the child. Then when the child performs the social skill, a sticker or star is placed directly on the tag, thus allowing the child to receive ongoing feedback on specific goal performance. The display of individual student goals helps the child and also reminds the adults in the learning environment to prompt the child to meet the goal.

Graham, Harris, and Reid (1992) offer guidelines for the most effective use of goal setting:

1. *Specificity.* Goals should be defined in specific (e.g., offer to share with one person during free play) versus more global terms (e.g., cooperate).

2. *Difficulty.* The goal defined should be challenging to the child but one that he or she can attain with reasonable effort. For example, a child who is often the recipient of taunting and teasing from peers may not initially be successful in Dealing with Teasing (Skill 27) on the playground at recess. Instead, a more achievable goal for the child may be to use the skill Asking for Help (Skill 6) or Ignoring (Skill 8) during free play in the classroom, where the teacher is available for ongoing support and guidance.

3. *Proximity.* The goal selected should be achievable within a reasonable time (the next hour, the same day, the same evening). This is particularly important for the young child.

In addition, the child should be prompted or reminded of his or her individual goal shortly before the opportunity to use the skill presents itself and should receive feedback and positive reinforcement as soon as the goal has been achieved.

Social skills games. A variety of games can be developed and used to enhance skill learning. Group games, in and of themselves, require students to practice a variety of social skills (e.g., joining in, sharing, being a good sport). Types of games that lend themselves well to Skillstreaming include board games and role-playing games. Cartledge and Milburn (1980) make several points worth considering when using social skills games:

FIGURE **13**   **Savannah's Goal-Setting Card**

Name ___Savannah_____ Date ___9/28/03____

My Goal

Following Directions (#10)

1. Listen.
2. Think about it.
3. Ask if needed.
4. Do it.

1. The connection between performing a skill in the game setting and in real life must be made explicit.

2. The winner (if there is one) should be determined on the basis of performance, rather than chance.

3. If rewards are used, they should be given for appropriate (skilled) participation, rather than winning.

4. Participants should not be "out" in a game without provisions for being allowed to participate again within a short period of time.

5. If teaming is required, skill-deficient children should be included on the same team as skill-competent children.

Skill folders. All students in the Skillstreaming group or classroom should keep a prosocial skills folder. This is simply a way of organizing materials—Skill Cards, homework assignments, awards, self-monitoring forms, and the like. Children will then have a readily available record of the behavioral steps of the skills they have practiced in the past. To enhance the likelihood that these prosocial behaviors will also be used outside of the instructional setting, the teacher may send the child's skills folder home on a regular basis. When parents communicate that the child demonstrates prosocial behaviors at home, Parent Awards can be inserted.

Beyond the Skillstreaming Session

The generalization-enhancing techniques examined thus far are directed toward the individual child. But maintenance and generalization of appropriate behaviors also may be enhanced by efforts directed toward others, especially those in the child's natural environment who function as the main providers of reinforcement.

Programming for reinforcement in the natural environment

The child's interpersonal world includes a variety of people— parents, siblings, peers, teachers, neighbors, and others. By their responsiveness or unresponsiveness to the child's newly learned skills, to a large extent these people control the destiny of these behaviors. We all react to what the important people in our lives think or feel about our behavior. What they reward, we are more likely to continue doing. What they are indifferent or hostile to will tend to fall into disuse.

During the past several years, we and others have suggested the increased involvement of educators, agency and institutional staff, parents, and peers in youths' acquisition and maintenance of prosocial skills. Parents in particular have been a second target for procedures designed to enhance the likelihood that prosocial skills, once learned, will be maintained. Chapter 10 offers a rationale and detailed procedures for involving parents in this very important work. Research suggests that parent training, as well as training of others significant in the child's life, enhances the child's own skill use.

Using natural reinforcers

A final and especially valuable approach to maintenance enhancement is the use of reinforcers that occur naturally in the child's environment. As Stokes and Baer (1977) observe:

Perhaps the most dependable of all generalization programming mechanisms is the one that hardly deserves
the name: the transfer of behavioral control from the
teacher-experimenter to stable, natural contingencies
that can be trusted to operate in the environment to
which the subject will return, or already occupies. To a
considerable extent, this goal is accomplished by choosing behaviors to teach that normally will meet maintaining reinforcement after the teaching. (p. 353)

Alberto and Troutman (1982) suggest a four-step process to
facilitate the use of natural reinforcers:

1. Observe which specific behaviors are regularly reinforced
   and how they are reinforced in the major settings that constitute the student's natural environment.

2. Instruct the student in a selected number of naturally reinforced
   behaviors (e.g., certain social skills, grooming behaviors).

3. Teach the student how to recruit or request reinforcement
   (e.g., by tactfully asking peers or others for approval or recognition).

4. Because its presence in certain gestures or facial expressions
   may be quite subtle, teach the student how to recognize reinforcement when it is offered.

SUMMARY

Although the technology described in this chapter is still evolving,
the call for transfer and maintenance enhancers has been largely
answered. We recommend the use of all of these strategies in
Skillstreaming instruction. We also contend that skill generalization
will be further promoted if the child is concurrently instructed in
the supportive psychological competencies previously discussed
in chapter 7 (i.e., problem solving, accurate perception of social situations, and verbal mediation).

CHAPTER 9
Managing Behavior Problems

Problems can and do occur in the Skillstreaming group, just as they may in any group-teaching endeavor. Some young children may prefer to engage in an unrelated activity and therefore not be motivated to participate. Others may actively resist involvement in group instruction. Still others may fail to see why the skills are important in their everyday lives. Their resistive behavior may interfere not only with their skill acquisition, but also with the learning of others in the group. This chapter describes a variety of management techniques for use with typical problem behaviors encountered during Skillstreaming instruction.

Once a management problem has been identified, the task becomes to select and implement one or more techniques to foster more desirable behavior. We do not suggest that only certain techniques be used with specific types of problem behavior. Just as one type of reinforcer may be rewarding for one child but not for another, a particular management strategy is likely to be more effective for one child than for another. Therefore, we will describe a range of strategies to be used when conducting Skillstreaming groups and urge that teachers and other group leaders individualize these methods, first using the least intrusive techniques.

Suggested strategies for managing behavioral concerns are described in the following four sections, moving from the least intrusive interventions (e.g., those strategies that are often effective, detract least from ongoing teaching efforts, and draw the least attention to the individual child) to individualized interventions. These sections concern the learning climate, supportive interventions, group management, behavior management techniques, and individual interventions.

LEARNING CLIMATE

The atmosphere of the Skillstreaming group, and the classroom, should be positive and encouraging. In other words, the teacher should openly notice the children following group rules, making prosocial choices, and "being good," rather than focus on catching them breaking rules. A benefit of this approach is that when teachers see children behaving appropriately and state approval of that behavior publicly, children engaging in unacceptable behavior are likely to stop problem behaviors and engage in the behaviors that received teacher approval (Kounin, 1970). Effectively managing ongoing classroom activities, creating structure and routines, and defining and enforcing behavioral expectations through classroom or group rules are ways of establishing an encouraging and supportive setting for learning.

Physical Structure

The physical environment can structure the learning setting. Most preschool and kindergarten classrooms have areas designed for a variety of free-play activities and learning activities (e.g., learning centers). To minimize potential behavior problems during teaching, the area in which Skillstreaming instruction is carried out needs to be large enough so children can participate in role plays without disrupting other group participants. Chairs or carpet samples for the children to sit on can help create physical distance between the children. To reduce distractions, enticing activities such as sand or water tables should be moved out of the group's view. The group rules, or behavioral guidelines, should be posted as a reminder for the entire group to use positive behavior.

In the classroom in general, allowing space for traffic can minimize disruption of ongoing activities as children move from one area to another. Increasing the physical structure of the group setting or classroom with strategies like those just described can minimize and avert many behavior problems; the structure can then be gradually lessened as the children become more familiar with working together.

Schedules or Routines

The teacher should provide a structure by creating a daily schedule of events. Within this schedule, the teacher sets the time for group instruction in Skillstreaming and plans opportunities to practice the prosocial skills the children have learned in the formal group setting. For example, if the skill is Waiting Your Turn (Skill 16), activities in which the children will need to take their turns, such as completing a puzzle as a group or drawing a group picture, can be planned. Most preschool and kindergarten teachers find it helpful to follow the same general schedule each day. Although special activities may occasionally alter the schedule, young children often feel more secure when they have a predictable daily routine. Providing a schedule of the school day in picture format and reviewing the schedule at the beginning of the school day can help avert many of the problems associated with changes in routine.

Structure in the form of routine is important within the Skillstreaming sessions as well. Although most young children quickly learn the pattern of Skillstreaming activities, it is helpful at the beginning of each session to let children know what activities will be taking place (e.g., "We'll show you the skill of Waiting Your Turn, then some of you will get a chance or to try it"). Informing the children of the specific activities they will be participating in will help prepare them for learning.

Defining Expectations (Rules)

Communicating classroom expectations is a critical aspect of providing effective structure. This is most clearly and easily done by establishing group guidelines or rules for acceptable behavior. Such rules should be reasonable ones that inform the children of what to do rather than forbid unacceptable behaviors. Establishing clearly defined rules in the early stages of group work may prevent many behavior problems and allows teachers to redirect the children in an encouraging and supportive manner.

Rules are guidelines governing appropriate and inappropriate student behaviors; procedures are what students need to know and follow to meet their own personal needs and perform routine instructional and classroom housekeeping activities. Teachers in supportive classrooms teach rules and procedures as explicitly as they teach academic content. Effective teachers integrate their rules and procedures—as well as consequences for not following them—into their classroom routines.

A number of effective "rules for the use of rules" have emerged in the behavior management literature (Greenwood, Hops, Delquadri, & Guild, 1974; Sarason, Glaser, & Fargo, 1972; Walker, 1979), including the following:

1. Define and communicate rules for student behavior in clear, specific, and, especially, behavioral terms. As Walker (1979) notes, it is better (more concrete and behavioral) to say, "Raise your hand before asking a question" than "Be considerate of others." A statement such as "Be kind or considerate of others" is a good goal, but too abstract. Instead, student behaviors should be clearly defined and phrased in a manner that students will understand, such as "Wait until another person has finished talking before you begin" and "Leave toys and other objects at your desk."

2. It is more effective to tell students what to do than what not to do. For example, if it is necessary to address aggression, instead of "No pushing or shoving," the rule should be phrased as "Keep hands and feet to yourself." Other positive examples include "Talk over disagreements" instead of "No fighting" and "Work quietly" instead of "Don't talk out of turn."

3. Rules should be communicated in a manner that will help students remember them. Depending upon the age group and rule difficulty, memorization aids may include keeping rules short and few in number (four or five rules is a workable number to use in most preschool and kindergarten classrooms), repeating the rules several times, and posting the rules in written and picture form in the classroom, as well as sending these guidelines home to parents. Rules should be reviewed at the beginning of each Skillstreaming session until all children remember them. Periodic review of rules may also be needed.

4. Following the rules is more likely when students have had a role in rule development, modification, and implementation.

However, often school and classroom rules are established by a committee of adults without student participation. Allowing the group to participate encourages the children's commitment to abide by the rules. Students can be asked to think of behaviors they feel they need to work together. It has been our experience, and that of many other practitioners, that students will state many rules that group leaders themselves would have identified. At times, more specific guidance may be needed, ideally in the form of leading questions, such as "Would everyone have a chance to be heard if everyone talked at once?" or "How might you let the leader know that you have something you want to say?"

5. In addition to the preceding ideas, further effective rules for rules are that (a) they be developed before group instruction begins; (b) they be fair, reasonable, and within students' capacity to follow; (c) that all members of the group understand them; and (d) they be applied consistently and fairly to all group members.

As is the case for rules, classroom procedures need to be explicitly taught; one cannot assume that students will know them without instruction. Unlike rules, which need to be taught "up front," procedures (e.g., for obtaining help, leaving the room, using rest room passes, sharpening pencils, handing in class work) usually can be explained as the need arises. However, procedures also will need to be clearly stated, closely monitored, consistently followed, retaught when necessary, and consequated when not followed.

SUPPORTIVE INTERVENTIONS

The Skillstreaming curriculum will be more readily learned by young children when presented in an encouraging and supportive environment. The previous section described considerations related to planning and structuring such a learning environment. The following interventions are designed to support children's desirable behaviors in an unobtrusive manner within the actual teaching sequence. These interventions include group teaching techniques, enhancing motivation, modifying antecedents, simplifying, prompting, surface management, behavioral redirection, and relationship-based techniques.

Group Teaching Techniques

What do teachers actually do to support positive behaviors in the learning setting? Kounin's (1970) observations, as well as our own (Goldstein, Palumbo, Striepling, & Voutsinas, 1995) suggest some important teacher behaviors. First, the teacher knows what is going on. Such *with-it-ness* is communicated to the class in a number of ways, including swift and consistent recognition and, when necessary, consequating of low-level behaviors likely to grow into disruptiveness or more serious aggression. Closely connected to such attentiveness is *overlapping,* the ability to manage simultaneously two or more classroom events, whether instructional or disciplinary. *Smoothness,* the ability to transition from one activity to another without "downtime," is a third facilitative teacher behavior. Downtime is a time for students to become bored and act out; avoiding or minimizing downtime significantly deters such behaviors.

Another way to minimize boredom is by instructing with *momentum,* maintaining a steady progress or movement throughout a particular lesson, class, or school day. A *group focus,* the ability to keep the entire class involved in a given instructional activity, also diminishes the likelihood of student aggression. Finally, an especially significant contributor to a supportive learning environment is the teacher's communication of *optimistic expectations.* Students live up to (and, unfortunately, also down to) what important people in their lives expect of them. The teacher who expects a child to be a "slow learner" or a "behavior problem" because of his or her past record, a sibling's past poor performance, or the neighborhood the student comes from will likely be rewarded with low performance or behavior problems. By contrast, the teacher who lets the student know he or she can achieve and will have the teacher's help along the way is likely to motivate the student to be more successful and less disruptive. The message is, expect the best of your students—you may well get it!

Consistent application of rules and procedures provides clear expectations for student behavior and establishes that the teacher is in charge of the classroom. Yet such consistency is difficult to maintain over time. Teachers become tired, overworked, and distracted. When this occurs, students are quick to get the message that perhaps "just this once" can become more than once. Then the boundary between what is and is not acceptable is no longer clear. Young children test the limits in order to reestablish the boundary, and, as this happens, the foundation for a supportive learning environment begins to erode.

Supportive environments are predictable environments. As noted previously, a well-thought-out and fairly and consistently enforced set of school rules or guidelines strongly helps establish such predictability. Consistent enforcement means that all staff are aware of and enforce rules in agreed-upon ways. But the demands of fairness and consistency may be contradictory at times. Consistency requires rule enforcement for all applicable occasions; fairness may require taking special circumstances into account and not enforcing a given rule in some instances.

Enhancing Motivation

Two types of motivators are typically employed to increase a child's use of desired behaviors. *Extrinsic motivators* are tangible rewards provided contingent upon performance of a desired skill or behavior. Such rewards take many forms. In the early years of the behavior modification movement, the use of extrinsic, tangible reinforcers was sometimes denounced as "bribery." The child, it was asserted, should want to engage in the desired behavior for its own sake and not for the external rewards it will bring. Some intervenors still offer such protests (e.g., Kohn, 1986), but most agree that the use of a combination of external and internal motivators is the most effective motivational strategy.

Tangible motivators are widely used in American schools and other settings serving children and youth. The stars and stickers of the preschool and kindergarten years take the form of points and special privileges and activities in the later grades. Extrinsic rewards appear to be especially useful in eliciting initial involvement in learning unfamiliar skills.

It has been the consistent experience of many teachers of Skillstreaming, however, that using only external rewards—whether in the form of tangible reinforcers or other incentives—is insufficient to sustain learning. We and others believe that substantial payoffs must be inherent in the activity itself. In Skillstreaming, such *intrinsic motivators* reside within the skills themselves, especially those that children choose themselves and use successfully in real-world settings. When children have the opportunity to select the skills they feel they need, they are more motivated to participate. When such student-selected (or, perhaps to a somewhat lesser degree, teacher-selected) skills yield positive outcomes in interactions with family, peers, or significant others, motivation is further enhanced.

In addition to regularly allowing children to select the skills for instruction, we have used a second tactic to augment intrinsic motivation. It is to communicate to the children, both during the initial structuring of the Skillstreaming group and periodically as the sessions unfold, that the goal of Skillstreaming is to teach alternatives, not substitutes. Many children who participate have been admonished, reprimanded, and punished literally hundreds of times for behaviors their parents, teachers, or others deemed inappropriate. In one way or another, they have been told, "Stop doing that, and do this instead" (e.g., "Stop talking and listen" or "Stop hitting and talk out the problem").

When teachers encounter preacademic or academic skill deficits in young children, they quickly understand the need to teach the child the necessary skills. For example, if a child has learned an inappropriate response (such as giving the sound of long *o* when shown the letter *a*), it is understood that additional instruction in that specific skill must occur. At this point, the child must both unlearn the inappropriate response and learn the correct response. The same is true when dealing with children's undesirable behaviors. The most successful means of decreasing a child's inappropriate behavior is to expand the child's behavioral repertoire, or range of possible responses. For example, if the child loses at a game with a peer, and the only response to losing he or she has learned, practiced, and been rewarded for is hitting, the child will hit again. The child has, in effect, no choices. If Skillstreaming teaches the child that losing may also be responded to by talking about feelings or making a coping statement (e.g., "Everybody can't win"), at least some of the time the child may use one of the more desirable responses in lieu of aggression. The very fact that reprimands, punishments, and the like have had to be used hundreds of times is testimony to their ineffectiveness. If the child has skill-response choices, then, when encouraged, prompted, and rewarded for using the skill choice, the chance is greater that he or she will, at least some of the time, use the skill in the future.

Modifying Antecedents

Addressing antecedents, or what appears to elicit problem behaviors, is an effective way to minimize these behavior problems. As discussed in chapter 1, children come to the structured preschool or kindergarten setting with a variety of skills, abilities, and prior experiences. Jones and Jones (1998) address modifications of antecedents related to academic achievement, including adjusting time, the learning environment, content (type, difficult, amount, or sequence), and organization. Such modifications of academic task antecedents are appropriate in the Skillstreaming process as well.

Children's abilities to handle particular group participation tasks will vary. Some may have difficulty following a series of instructions or understanding the meaning of specific concepts included in the directions. For these children, it would be helpful to present fewer instructions at a time or to repeat instructions, rephrasing them in language that the children can more easily understand. In addition, any task may be divided into a sequence of steps that the children can perform one at a time.

Simplifying

Simplifying, or asking less at one time, is another way to increase the likelihood that students will experience success in the Skillstreaming group. Children's abilities to handle particular group tasks will vary. Some may have difficulty following a series of instructions, understanding instructions, or knowing what to say during feedback time. Methods of simplifying include the following:

- Have the student role-play one behavioral step at a time. Reward minimal student accomplishment.

- Shorten the role play.

- Coach the child through a prepared script that visually portrays the behavioral steps.

- Ask the student to take the role of coactor before that of main actor.

Prompting

The teacher needs to anticipate problems in the classroom or Skillstreaming session and then prompt desired behaviors. Prompting, or telling the child what to do in a given situation, can minimize behavior problems and also provides a positive, encouraging environment in which to foster learning. For example, if a group of five children are each given paper and scissors but are given only two bottles of glue, it is important for the teacher to anticipate the problem of sharing the glue. Once specific Skillstreaming skills are learned, the skills themselves can be used to prompt desired behaviors. In the preceding scenario, for example, the teacher might remind the group of the steps to Sharing (Skill 17) or Asking a Favor (Skill 7).

During Skillstreaming instruction, one of the teacher's main functions is to anticipate difficulties and be ready to prompt a desirable response during role-play activities. Children practicing a new skill in a session may easily forget a step or several steps, or they may not know how to behave in order to carry out a particular skill step. The teacher may then give instructional comments or hints to elicit the behavior (e.g., "We heard you think about your choices. Now you're going to make a choice") or coach the student from start to finish. Prompting may also prevent the child from acting in a disruptive or aggressive manner out of fear of failing. Such coaching will help the child practice performing the skill steps correctly, rather than experiencing additional failure.

Surface Management

Several techniques for unobtrusively managing mild and commonly occurring misbehaviors have been suggested by Redl and Wineman (1957). These methods, termed *surface management* techniques, have been used successfully to deal with problem behaviors in Skillstreaming groups.

Planned ignoring

Mild misbehaviors can best be dealt with by simply ignoring them. Many times, drawing attention to such behaviors is more distracting to the learning process than the behaviors themselves. Positively reinforcing concurrent appropriate behavior helps eliminate the inappropriate action. This strategy is most effective when the group leader plans in advance which mild behaviors will be ignored.

> **EXAMPLE.** Susie often played with the laces on her new shoes during the Skillstreaming sessions, despite the fact that the teacher had taken her aside prior to the group's beginning to ask that she sit cross-legged and keep her hands away from her shoes. Because Susie's behavior did not appear to distract others in the group, the teacher decided to ignore the behavior to see if, with lack of attention, the behavior would diminish.

Proximity control

In proximity control, the teacher moves closer to (stands near, sits next to) the student who is misbehaving. Often simply moving closer to the student who is engaging in problematic or distracting behavior will draw the student's attention back to the learning situation. For students who do not mind being touched, a hand on the shoulder is an effective way of drawing the student back to task.

> **EXAMPLE.** While the group was providing feedback to the role players, Judy began singing. The leader quietly moved away from the front of the group, stood next to Judy, and touched her shoulder while continuing to elicit feedback about the role play.

Signal interference

Signal interference includes nonverbal communicators that let the child know a behavior is unacceptable. This may include eye contact, hand gestures, or clearing one's throat. Some students who engage in mildly disruptive behavior may not even realize they are doing something distracting to others. In such cases, prearranging with the child a specific signal (e.g., a word or gesture) to cue the child that the behavior is occurring has been a useful strategy.

EXAMPLE. While the teacher modeled the skill, Enrique began playing with Samantha's hair, distracting her from the modeling display. The teacher caught Enrique's eye, shook her head no, and continued with the modeling.

Interest boosting

When a student's attention appears to be drifting away from an activity, it is often helpful to boost the child's interest. This can be done by involving the child more directly in the activity, asking for his or her input, or directing a high-interest question to the group.

EXAMPLE. While the teacher was generating situations where the skill could be used, Cody became restless, turning around and trying to engage others in conversation. The teacher, changing her tone of voice to one of anticipation, asked the group if they had experienced similar situations. To increase the interest of all children, the teacher asked for a thumbs-up or thumbs-down as a response.

Humor

At times, something very clever or humorous may be expressed by a student in the Skillstreaming group. Such a humorous moment can quickly ease a tense situation. As long as the humor is not at the expense of a specific individual or group, or the child is not being rewarded for being a class clown, it is fine to go ahead and laugh.

EXAMPLE. While the group was getting ready to begin, one child told a silly knock-knock joke, and all the other group members laughed. Instead of reprimanding the child, the teacher laughed along with the others for a few moments and then began the instruction.

Restructuring the classroom program

Sometimes the class schedule must be abandoned in favor of dealing with a problem that has just occurred. If students appear tense and upset due to a playground problem, for example, requiring them to practice a less immediately relevant skill will not meet their needs. Instead, the teacher should abandon the preplanned lesson and restructure the lesson, changing the skill to be taught.

Capturing such teachable moments can take the form of employing Skillstreaming to better manage the instructional setting. Many problem behaviors—including withdrawal, disruptiveness, threats, and so forth—may be viewed as behavioral excess: too much talking, too much bullying, and so on. However, basic behaviors may equally well be construed as behavioral deficiencies: too little listening to others, too little concern for others, and so on. Thus an additional way to reduce problem behaviors is to replace them with desirable ones. The Skillstreaming curriculum consists of just such alternatives. Skills may be taught as previously scheduled (as part of regular sessions) or at spontaneous times that help students reduce behavior problems (i.e., teachable moments).

> **EXAMPLE.** Following recess, several children in the class were visibly agitated, and two children had been crying. After questioning the class, the teacher learned that some of the children had been bullied by an older child, and the playground supervisor hadn't seen the problem. Even though the teacher's plan for the day was to work on a different skill, he abandoned this plan and introduced the more timely skill of Knowing When to Tell (Skill 35) to encourage the children to tell the playground supervisor the next time.

Removing seductive objects

It is natural for children to be distracted by interesting objects and toys. Including the group guideline of leaving toys and other objects at one's desk may prevent such distractions from occurring during Skillstreaming sessions.

> **EXAMPLE.** Antonio brought a new toy to the group and began showing it to others. The teacher asked Antonio to finish showing the toy and then directed him to put it either in his desk or in her desk for safekeeping.

Taking a break

When a child's behavior is not easily controlled within the teaching setting, it may be best for the child to take a break. Redl and Wineman (1957) describe this approach as "antiseptic bouncing." This measure is not intended to be punitive, but rather to remove the child from a situation before he or she loses control. With this technique, the child is asked to leave the room to get a drink of water, run an errand, and so forth.

> **EXAMPLE.** Joshua couldn't seem to settle down despite the teacher's attempts to involve him. The teacher quietly called Joshua away from the group, said she had neglected to take a folder to the director's office, and requested that he help her out by immediately delivering the folder.

Reality appraisal

This technique involves giving students an explanation of why a behavior is not acceptable, or "telling it like it is." This approach, which helps children understand the consequences of their behavior, is most effective if the teacher or group leader has established a positive relationship with the children in the group.

> **EXAMPLE.** During feedback, most of the children began talking all at once. The group leader responded, "If everyone talks at once, we won't be able to hear anyone's ideas."

Behavioral Redirection

One way to encourage a student's appropriate behavior while preventing the occurrence of negative actions is to employ behavioral redirection. This means calling the child's attention to a different task or activity, thus directing him away from the inappropriate behavior or action. For example, a student who frequently disrupts the Skillstreaming sessions by standing up and wandering around the room may be asked to help the teacher by pointing to the skill steps as they are being role-played. Another example might be to request that a child who inappropriately brings toys to the group take other classroom materials and put them on the teacher's desk, replacing the toy on the way. Still another student who has difficulty keeping her hands to herself might be asked to sit next to the teacher and hold the box of props needed for the role play.

Relationship-Based Techniques

Psychologists and educators have long known that the better the relationship between the helper and client (student), the more positive and productive the outcome of their interaction. In fact, it has been demonstrated that a positive relationship is a potent factor in effecting long-term behavior change. The techniques next described draw primarily upon the relationship between teacher and student, and can often be combined with other management techniques for maximum effect. Two such techniques, especially useful when working with young children, are empathic encouragement and threat reduction.

Empathic encouragement

Empathic encouragement is a strategy in which the teacher first shows that he or she understands the difficulty the child is experiencing and then urges the child to participate as instructed. Often this additional one-to-one attention will motivate the child to participate and follow the teacher's guidance. In applying this technique, the teacher first listens to the child's explanation of the problem and expresses an understanding of the child's feelings and behavior (e.g., "I know it seems difficult to learn something new"). If appropriate, the teacher responds that the child's view is valid. The teacher then restates his or her own view with supporting reasons and outcomes, and urges the child to try out the suggestion (e.g., "If you don't try it, you won't know that you can do it. Let's just try").

Threat reduction

This technique is helpful in dealing with children's anxiety. Children who find role-playing or other types of participation threatening may react with inappropriate or disruptive behaviors, or withdraw from the learning process. To deal with this problem, the teacher should provide reassurance or even physical contact (e.g., an arm around the child, a pat on the back). The teacher should also encourage group members to express support for the role player and others who participate.

Other strategies for threat reduction include postponing the student's role-playing until last and clarifying and restructuring those aspects of the task that the student experiences as threatening. Simplifying and coaching may also help the child become more willing to engage in the learning activity.

GROUP MANAGEMENT

Strong teachers use the techniques and strategies just described in all types of teaching situations. Such nonintrusive, supportive interventions communicate positive expectations for children and effectively remediate the majority of behavioral problems that occur in Skillstreaming instruction. There are times, however, that some groups of children do not receive enough support from the learning climate and supportive interventions to be successful in changing their behavior. In such cases, group management strategies are needed. The following plan has often been found useful in working with difficult groups of young children.

Step 1: Reward positive behavior

Foremost among behavior management techniques for dealing with problematic behavior in the classroom is positive reinforcement. Many disruptions can be reduced or even eliminated by applying positive reinforcement to such desirable classroom behaviors as listening, participating, and following group guidelines. Positive reinforcement also has a powerful effect on children who are behaving inappropriately if children who are engaging in desirable behavior are rewarded. For example, if those who are listening are reinforced with verbal praise, a ripple effect is created, and the inattentive children will most likely begin to listen as well (Kounin, 1970). This strategy allows the teacher to control the group in a positive, helping way and decreases the impulse to nag children to pay attention.

Step 2: Offer positive consequences

Reminding students of the positive consequences of desirable behavior will often encourage them to stop an undesirable behavior and engage in the more desirable one. Offering positive consequences means telling students that a specific desirable behavior will earn a given reward. Examples include "When you listen, you may have a turn" and "When you put your materials away, you may join the group." Some behaviors may need a tangible positive consequence: "When you wait your turn, you'll earn your ticket (or sticker or star)." Reminding students to engage in a specific appropriate behavior to earn a privilege or reward lets them know that positive actions lead to good things—and it does so in an encouraging, helpful manner. It is important to present the positive consequences for stopping an undesirable action before informing children of any negative consequences.

Step 3: Inform of negative consequences

The majority of minor behavioral difficulties (e.g., inattention, noisemaking) will likely be remedied by employing Steps 1 and 2 of this plan. However, if a child's inappropriate behavior does not cease, it may be necessary to inform him or her of the negative consequences of continuing the undesirable behavior. Examples of negative consequences include sitting away from the group for a minute, not earning stickers or other rewards that have been structured within the classroom plan, or not receiving a privilege such as extra recess time. Consequences should be as logically related to the misbehavior as possible. For example, if the child misuses classroom materials, he or she would then lose the privilege of using these materials for the rest of the day. Informing the child of negative consequences thus provides a warning of what will happen if the child continues to engage in that behavior. It is important for the teacher to have thought in advance of logically linked consequences that match the severity of the misbehavior. Thinking ahead in such a manner will prevent the application of consequences that are impossible to enforce or too severe.

Step 4: Allow choice

After being informed of both positive and negative consequences, the child is instructed to make a choice—either stop the behavior and earn the positive reinforcement or continue the behavior and accept the negative consequences. When a child is given a choice, power struggles are eliminated. We cannot make a child behave in the way we would like the child to behave; however, we can structure the consequences to encourage the child to make socially acceptable choices.

It is often helpful to allow the child time to make the choice. Informing the child that he or she will have 2 minutes to make the choice to put materials away or 1 minute to make the choice of whether or not to stop disrupting the group allows the teacher to leave the child alone, lessens the potential for a power struggle, reinforces the idea that the child can control both positive and negative consequences, and allows the child to maintain his or her dignity.

Step 5: Enforce positive or negative consequences

Either positive or negative consequences are next carried out. If the child chooses negative consequences by continuing the undesirable behavior, these are delivered in a calm and firm manner. For example, if the child continues to disrupt the Skillstreaming group by making noises, and the consequence for this is to sit away from the group for 2 or 3 minutes, then the child is required to follow through. Once a negative consequence has been enforced, the teacher should reevaluate the structure of the learning environment, making supportive accommodations for the student—for example, seating the child closer to a group leader or implementing a structured management plan based on positive reinforcement (e.g., for meeting the goal of listening in the group, receiving stickers that can be traded for 5 minutes of free play following the group).

If the child makes the choice to stop the behavior as requested, then the child should receive the positive consequence (e.g., allowing the child to remain in the group or continue to use class materials). It is important to stress that once a child has earned a reward for a given positive behavior (e.g., stickers for listening), the reward should not be taken away as a negative consequence for another undesirable behavior. Loss of a reward previously earned may result in more severe maladaptive behavior, such as aggression or loss of motivation to earn the reward.

> EXAMPLE. When Sam began disrupting the group by making silly comments and laughing, the group leader rewarded those children who had been listening by giving verbal praise and "participation tickets" (Step 1). Sam

continued the behavior, and the teacher responded, "Sam, when you show that you are listening, you may have your turn to role-play" (Step 2). Sam stopped the comments and laughing, and at the completion of the ongoing role play, Sam received his turn. If he had continued, the teacher would have calmly walked over to him, saying privately, "Sam, you need to stop the silly comments. It's distracting all of us. If you stop, you'll have the opportunity to role-play and earn your tickets for free time (Step 2). "If you don't stop, you'll need to do a time-out" (Step 3). If Sam persisted, the teacher would say, "You need to choose. I'll set the timer for 2 minutes" (Step 4). Depending on the choice Sam made, the teacher would follow through with the positive or negative consequence (Step 5).

BEHAVIOR MANAGEMENT TECHNIQUES

Behavior management techniques (i.e., behavior modification) both promote skill learning and inhibit problematic behaviors. The effectiveness of behavior modification technology rests upon a firm, well-validated foundation.

Beyond the repeated demonstration of their effectiveness, behavior modification techniques are relatively easy to learn and use; may be administered by the teacher, parent, peers, or the child; and have a long history of successful use. For these reasons, the techniques can maximize time and opportunity for student learning.

Reinforcement

A major way to substitute appropriate for inappropriate behaviors is to present positive reinforcement to the student following and contingent upon the occurrence of appropriate behavior. A positive reinforcer is any event that increases the subsequent frequency of a behavior it follows. Teachers and other school-based contingency managers have worked successfully with four types of positive reinforcers: material, social, activity, and token.

Material reinforcers (sometimes called *tangible reinforcers*) are actual objects presented to the individual contingent upon the enactment of appropriate behaviors. A specific type of material reinforcer is the skill award (see Figures 10, 11, and 12, on pages 176, 177, and 178, for examples). An important subcategory of material reinforcement, *primary reinforcement,* occurs when the contingent event presented satisfies a basic biological need. Food is one such primary reinforcer.

Social reinforcers—most often expressed in the form of attention, praise, or approval—are particularly powerful and are frequently used in the Skillstreaming group. Both teacher experience and extensive experimental research testify to the potency of social reinforcement in influencing a broad array of personal, interpersonal, and academic student behaviors.

Activity reinforcers are those events the child freely chooses when an opportunity exists to engage in several different activities. Given freedom to choose, many children will watch television rather than complete their homework. The parent wishing to use this activity reinforcer may specify that the child may watch television for a given time period contingent upon the prior completion of the homework. Stated otherwise, the opportunity to perform a higher probability behavior (given free choice) can be used as a reinforcer for a lower probability behavior.

Token reinforcers, usually employed when more easily implemented social reinforcers prove insufficient, are symbolic items (chips, stars, stickers, etc.) provided contingent upon the performance of appropriate or desirable behaviors. Tokens thus obtained are exchangeable for a wide range of material or activity reinforcers. A *token economy* is a system by which specific numbers of tokens are contingently gained and exchanged for the backup material or activity reinforcers.

In deciding which type of reinforcer to use with a given youngster, the teacher should keep in mind that social reinforcement (e.g., attention, praise, approval) is easiest to implement on a continuing basis and is most likely to lead to enduring behavior change. Therefore, it is probably the type of reinforcement the teacher will wish to use most frequently. Unfortunately, in the initial stages of a behavior-change effort—especially when aggressive, disruptive, and other inappropriate behaviors are probably being richly rewarded by teacher and peer attention, as well as by tangible reinforcers—the teacher will likely need to rely more on material and activity reinforcers.

The potency, or strength, of many reinforcers is increased when the reward, in addition to being inherently desirable, also brings reinforcement from peers and others (e.g., earning extra gym or recess time for the class). A further benefit of certain activity reinforcers (e.g., playing a game with peers) is the degree to which the activity, while serving as a reward, also helps the student practice one or more Skillstreaming skills. Table 4 presents a variety of material and social reinforcers appropriate for the preschool and kindergarten child.

Consequences

Children who frequently behave in their everyday lives in an angry, aggressive, bullying, and threatening manner may also do so in the Skillstreaming group. If such behaviors are not dealt with—immediately, swiftly, and successfully—other children are unlikely to participate in the group. The Skillstreaming teacher functions not only as an instructor, model, and role-play/feedback guide, but also as a protector. In creating a safe and supportive learning environment, the teacher must immediately correct any efforts to bully, intimidate, or otherwise treat others in an inappropriate, aggressive manner. Such vigilance and responsiveness not only serve to protect the victim but also, if done constructively, offer an additional teaching opportunity for the aggressor. No matter how skilled the leader is in modeling, conducting role-playing, and so forth, if the group is not safe, learning cannot take place.

Time-out

The immediate consequence most commonly used in preschool and kindergarten classrooms is time-out. Time-out is an extinction technique that involves removing the child from positive reinforcement (e.g., attention) when other forms of extinction (e.g., ignoring) have been unsuccessful. Most often, time-out involves removing the disruptive child from the ongoing activity to sit on a chair in a specified area of the classroom. This procedure should be used only after a child has been forewarned of the specific behaviors that will warrant its use and when other management techniques have failed. Time-out is a last resort because it removes the child not only from positive reinforcement, but also

TABLE 4 **Material and Social Reinforcers**

Material Reinforcers

Objects

Food (e.g., peanuts, raisins, apples, cereal, gum)

Stickers

Stars

Skill tickets

Happy faces

Awards

Good notes home

Ribbons

"Good work" buttons

Rubber stamp on hand

Small toy or trinket

Photo of child

Activities

Feeding pets

Watering plants

Being first in line

One-on-one time with teacher

Extra free play

Sharpening pencils

Playing with a special toy

Listening to a CD

Sitting at teacher's desk or chair

Extra outside play

Using teacher's equipment (e.g., stapler, hole punch)

Using colored chalk on chalkboard or sidewalk

Selecting a story to be read to the class

Earning a puzzle piece (completing the puzzle when all pieces are earned)

Listening to a story on video- or audiotape

Using the computer

Using the telephone

Social Reinforcers

Nonverbal

Smiling

Hugging

Looking interested

Physical closeness

A pat on the back

A wink

Nodding

Arm around the child

Holding hands

Verbal

Good listening, good thinking, and so forth

Thank you.

Wow!

I really like that.

That was nice.

You really waited.

Nice job!

Terrific!

Great work (or other behavior)!

from the learning environment. Furthermore, it must be recognized that time-out is only a signal to the child of the inappropriateness of his or her actions. Time-out may also provide relief to the teacher and other group members, but it does not teach the child alternative behaviors (Grant & Van Acker, 2000).

For the preschool or kindergarten child, the time-out condition should not exceed 2 or 3 minutes. This is long enough to convey to the child the inappropriateness of the behavior for which time-out is the consequence. Using time-out for longer than the recommended time will likely result in the child's exhibiting undesirable behavior while in time-out, which then requires further intervention. This teacher attention, even though negative, may be perceived by the child to be rewarding. Longer periods of time-out may also result in children's feeling that they don't belong, and they may later avoid the activities or settings in which they have been excluded (Grant & Van Acker, 2000). When the child returns to the instructional setting, it is critical that he or she receive positive reinforcement immediately for any type of appropriate behavior. The teacher must create an environment where the child wants to be, or the child may actually begin to see time-out as a positive alternative.

The responsible teacher or other group leader will plan instruction in specific skills that could serve as socially acceptable ways of dealing with the problem that led to the use of time-out. For example, the student could be guided through the steps of Solving a Problem (Skill 30) to reduce the likelihood that the event will reoccur. In addition, the teacher must attempt to deescalate future occurrences of such behavior through techniques like prompting the child through other relevant skills.

In some cases, a child may know he or she is emotionally unable to handle the classroom or group setting and may request a time-out or cooling-off period. Referred to by Grayson, Kiraly, and McKinnon (1996) as the *cooling-off approach,* this method allows the child to spend time alone in a nonstressful setting or time with an adult to discuss the child's concerns. This form of therapeutic crisis intervention may avert more serious behavioral difficulties. The teacher needs to monitor the child's use of cooling-off periods carefully to judge that they are not employed to avoid particular classroom activities, subjects, or Skillstreaming tasks.

EXAMPLE. Billy gradually became more agitated in the group. When the teacher inquired whether he was having a problem, Billy asked to sit on a rug in the reading area for a while. After 2 or 3 minutes, the teacher asked him if he was ready to return to the group.

Logical consequences versus punishment

It is a common finding that, when punishment does succeed in altering behavior, such effects are often temporary. In part because of this temporary effect, but more so for even more important reasons, a number of contingency management researchers have assumed an antipunishment stance, seeing little place for punishment, especially in the contemporary classroom. This view corresponds to punishment research demonstrating such undesirable side effects as withdrawal from social contact, counteraggression toward the punisher, modeling of punishing behavior, disruption of social relationships, failure of effects to generalize, selective avoidance (refraining from inappropriate behaviors only when under surveillance), and stigmatizing labeling effects (Azrin & Holz, 1966; Bandura, 1973).

An encouraging environment teaches students to respect themselves and others and ensures that all students are treated with dignity and respect. Rarely are students exposed to punishment; however, clear and consistent limits on unacceptable behavior are set and enforced so all children have the opportunity to learn. Such limits involve the administration of logical consequences. Logical consequences (Dreikurs & Cassel, 1972) differ from punishment in several important ways. Such consequences are related to the misbehavior (punishment rarely is); are planned, explained, and agreed upon by children in advance (there is often no forewarning with punishment); administered in a neutral, matter-of-fact way (not in anger, as punishment often is); and given consistently. In addition, they are reasonable and demonstrate respect by giving children a choice (i.e., engage in the inappropriate behavior and receive an unpleasant consequence, or engage in the appropriate behavior and receive a positive consequence).

When planning logical consequences, teachers will need to keep in mind that these consequences must be reasonable, related to the misbehavior, and respectful of the child (Nelsen, Lott, &

Glenn, 1993). Examples of logical consequences include the following:

- For choosing to talk instead of completing the center activity, the child must complete the center work during free time.

- For choosing to fight at recess, the child must stay on a specific area of the playground where there is increased supervision.

- For choosing to take a picture book belonging to someone else, the child makes restitution.

INDIVIDUAL INTERVENTIONS

Children who do not increase positive behaviors when provided with consistent structure and routines, along with supportive interventions and group management procedures, may require an individual behavior plan. A student for whom it is frequently necessary to use time-out, for example, will likely benefit from an individual behavior plan. Such a plan can be designed by following these steps:

1. Identify the behavior to be changed. To do this, list the student's problematic behaviors in concrete, observable, and measurable terms. Then choose one behavior to decrease in frequency. This may be the behavior that bothers you the most or the one creating the greatest problem for the student.

2. Obtain baseline data to determine how frequently, and under what conditions, the undesirable behavior occurs. This process need not be complicated. For example, you may list the undesirable behavior and make a tally mark for each occurrence of the behavior on a given day, generally assessing whether the day has been "typical" for the child. Or you may find an A–B–C format useful (specifying *antecedent* conditions under which the behavior occurred, the specific *behavior* exhibited by the child, and the *consequences* that the child receives as a result of that behavior). The A–B–Cs can be written on a sheet of paper and quickly documented whenever the behavior of concern is observed.

3. On the basis of the preceding assessment and including other assessment data as appropriate, hypothesize as to the function or purpose of the child's behavior (i.e., what that behavior achieves for the child). Instead of looking solely at the child's overt behavior (e.g., hitting, refusing, crying), ask what the child is accomplishing from this behavior. The answer to this question is a "best guess" about the function of the child's behavior. Typical functions for behavior problems that occur in school settings are to gain attention (e.g., from peers or adults), to escape or avoid (e.g., a task or person), or to gain access to something (e.g., a desired item or activity; Jolivette, Scott, & Nelson, 2000).

   Dreikurs, Grunwald, and Pepper (1971) offer four reasons for misbehavior: attention, power, revenge, and inadequacy. Is the child's goal to seek attention or to belong? To control the group? To ruin the teaching opportunity? To avoid participation? Perhaps the student is displaying the particular resistive behavior to avoid a task he perceives as too complicated (e.g., one that has too many steps). Another student may be experiencing anxiety as she realizes that her turn to role-play is approaching. Still another child may not be receiving the desired amount of attention from others. Another may engage in undesirable behaviors to belong and gain friends.

4. When you have identified what is motivating the child's behaviors (e.g., attention, escape, etc.), alternative or replacement behaviors can then be identified. The replacement behavior serves the same function or purpose as the undesirable behavior. For example, if the undesirable behavior is not following directions, the replacement behavior would be to follow directions.

5. Teach the replacement behavior.

6. Determine an effective reinforcer, and deliver it consistently when the replacement behavior occurs. If the reward is given immediately following the replacement behavior, it is more likely that the behavior will be repeated. Some small reinforcer (e.g., verbal encouragement, a sticker) should be given immediately following the behavior. A larger reward (e.g., a special privilege) may be given later—for example, when the child's sticker card is full.

7. Once the individual plan has been implemented, monitor behavior change. A chart or graph of the replacement behavior and the initial behavior of concern will show the degree of progress.

It is important to evaluate the child's progress. If, for example, the replacement behavior is not increasing (or the problem behavior is not decreasing), the plan must be altered. It could be, for instance, that the hypothesis about the problem behavior was incorrect, that the replacement behavior selected did not serve the same function for the child as the problem behavior, and so forth. Effective individual interventions are ones that work; as such, monitoring the effectiveness of the plan and making needed changes as indicated by the data are important aspects of behavior change.

SUMMARY

Problem behaviors in Skillstreaming groups are those that interfere with or detract from the group's process as an active, facilitative learning environment. A variety of techniques for dealing with specific types of problem behaviors have been described in this chapter. All of these techniques share the common goal of helping the child become actively involved in Skillstreaming so the skills can be learned, practiced, and rewarded.

CHAPTER 10

Parent Support

Parents often look to the schools for support, and schools increasingly have become a venue in which a wide variety of services for children and adolescents are provided (Dryfoos, 1994). For young children and their families, school is becoming a community resource, offering health-related and social service programming and often including parent support and training. Expansion of the role of schools is likely to continue. Within this framework, involving families in Skillstreaming is a way to enhance the community of support for the young child.

BUILDING POSITIVE RELATIONSHIPS WITH PARENTS

With very few exceptions, parents genuinely care about their children's academic and social progress as they enter the world of preschool and beyond. Often, cultural and socioeconomic differences impair the development of a common understanding between parents and teachers. Such misunderstandings are unfortunate and have the potential to put the social and emotional welfare of young children at risk. Although many teachers indicate that parent involvement is difficult to achieve, Skillstreaming is a productive and often nonemotional way to begin parent and school collaboration.

Traditionally, parent contact has taken the form of PTA meetings, parent-teacher conferences, or, as far too often has been the case with a child prone to behave aggressively or disruptively, the "bad news call." Teachers able to create positive relationships with parents often view and deal with parents quite differently. They demonstrate understanding of cultural and economic differences. They recognize and appreciate parents as the child's first (and continuing) teachers. They seek contact early and frequently, seeing this as an opportunity to collaborate in supportive, mutually reinforcing ways. Displaying such attitudes helps create the opportunity for the parent, teacher, and student to become a problem-solving team.

The role of parents and the family has gradually changed from being on the periphery to being a central focus in the child's education. It is more widely understood that establishing close working relationships with parents, in the early grades especially (e.g., kindergarten through third grade), can have a positive effect on the child's school adjustment (Strain & Timm, 2001; Walker et al., 1995). Opportunities for the child to be successful in school, home, and peer group increase with a cooperative working relationship between parents and the school.

Although there is an increased emphasis on expanding the role of the family in the young child's school experience (e.g., involving parents to a greater degree in decision making), teachers and other professionals may not be sufficiently prepared for such collaboration (Friesen & Stephens, 1998). A model for the development of positive and productive relationships presented by Fialka and Mikus (1999) may be helpful to the teacher or other Skillstreaming leader. This model calls for a partnership between home and school that can be developed through specific phases of parent-teacher interaction.

The first phase of relationship development, which Fialka and Mikus call *colliding and campaigning,* involves fostering understanding and beginning to build trust between parent and teacher. During this initial phase of relationship building, each party typically has difficulty listening to the other. Instead, it is often the goal to state their own perspectives about the child, the problem, or the intervention, with the hope of persuading the other to see the issue from their vantage point and to accept their solution. During initial parent contacts, then, it is important for each party to have the goal of listening for understanding, to ask for more information, and to be willing to explore different possibilities in resolving concerns.

With successful work at the first phase, parents and teachers move to the middle phase, *coordinating, cooperating, and compromising,* in which their interactions are based on more effective listening and cooperation. Being able to suspend their personal agendas to explore a common ground and asking each other to explain ideas will give rise to respect for the other and increased capacity for problem solving. *Collaborating and creative partnering,* the third phase of relationship building, continues to be based on listening and inquiring. During this phase, there is more open sharing of each party's needs, hopes, and fears. Differences of opinion are more easily understood and accepted, and decision making becomes more balanced between the parties. Although these phases are described as discrete, relationships will often move back and forth among the phases as parents and teachers engage in problem solving.

Emotional and behavioral problems affect the child in all life situations—home, neighborhood, school, church, and so forth. In addition, families experience significant stress when their child has emotional and behavioral problems. Collaboration between teacher and parent best addresses the child's behavioral and social needs. Communication with the student's family should, therefore, be one of the most important components of any school program (Quinn et al., 2000).

PARENTING AND CHILDREN'S AGGRESSION

Overall, parents do the best they can with what they know. However, parenting styles and practices significantly affect the young child's later school and social adjustment. Considerable research evidence suggests that children exhibiting aggression during the preschool years, for example, often have been exposed to harsh, punitive, rigid, and authoritarian discipline and parents who model aggression (Jewett, 1992). On the other hand, parenting practices related to prosocial behavior include appropriate and fair discipline, sufficient supervision, involvement in the child's life (e.g., school and peer contacts), an attitude of support, and the ability to resolve conflicts and handle crises in the family (Walker et al., 1995).

A 7-year follow-up study of parents of kindergarten children found that four types of parenting behavior promoted young children's later adjustment in school (Pettit, Bates, & Dodge, 2000). These positive parenting behaviors included warmth, supportive discipline (e.g., calm discussions), interest and involvement in the child's life (e.g., peer contacts), and the proactive teaching of social skills. In addition to promoting positive adaptation across the elementary school years, these parenting skills may also serve as a protective factor, buffering the risks associated with family stressors (e.g., financial stress, divorce).

PARENT INVOLVEMENT IN SKILLSTREAMING

Parents can and should be involved in Skillstreaming for a variety of important reasons. First, parenting practices may be at cross-purposes with what is taught in the school (Cartledge & Milburn, 1995). A specific skill taught in the Skillstreaming group may not be supported at home, and its use may actually be discouraged. For example, a young child's attempt to use the skill Knowing When to Tell (Skill 35) may be met with the parent response to "stop tattling." Such contradictions from important people in the child's life will be confusing and may discourage further use of the skill. When parents understand the goals of Skillstreaming, as well as the specific behaviors included, they are far more likely to be receptive to the child's skill initiations. Furthermore, because Skillstreaming provides a specific way of teaching children "what to do," the opportunity exists to alter how parents deal with the child's problems in the home and with peers and siblings. For example, when parents learn to reinforce and prompt prosocial skill use—and to change the consequences that maintain a child's aggression (Patterson, 1982)—more positive and supportive parenting will likely result. In this way, parent involvement and cooperation in Skillstreaming have the potential to improve parenting skills.

Second, many social and behavioral problems originate in the home setting (Walker et al., 1995). Therefore, the more settings in which prosocial skill use is prompted and rewarded, the greater the likelihood that the skills taught will be maintained and will generalize. As discussed in chapter 8, children may easily learn the Skillstreaming skills, but they are unlikely to continue to use skills over time or in a variety of situations and environments unless specific procedures are implemented to facilitate their use. Reinforcement and prompting of skill use in the home setting is a way to enhance continued use of learned skills.

A third rationale for including parents in Skillstreaming concerns the profound effect of modeling on the young child's behavior. When parents and siblings model behaviors for dealing with stress and anger, for example, the young child follows these models.

LEVELS OF INVOLVEMENT

In collaborating with parents on behalf of the young child, several goals are apparent. Cartledge and Milburn (1995) emphasize the value in conveying to parents the importance of social skills learning to the child's development, an awareness of the social skills needed to be successful outside the home, and actions they may take to assist the child in skill learning. The level of involvement will vary according to the receptivity of both parents and professionals. We recommend that the following levels be prescriptively matched to the needs of the child targeted for skills training.

Orientation Level

The first level of parent involvement can best be described as an orientation to Skillstreaming skills and procedures. The purpose of this level is to promote parent awareness and understanding. An orientation meeting to describe Skillstreaming objectives and ways parents might help their child use the prosocial skills at home is highly encouraged. Presenting examples of skills, discussing the goals of Skillstreaming, and explaining the learning process (modeling, role-playing, performance feedback, and homework), by showing *The Skillstreaming Video* (Goldstein & McGinnis, 1988) or conducting a mock group, are activities that will increase parent understanding. Allowing time for questions and input about skills for instruction will also increase parents' understanding and involvement.

An alternative to an orientation meeting is to send a letter home explaining the goals of Skillstreaming instruction and the activities in which the child will be participating (i.e., watching leaders act out a skill, trying out the skill steps in the group, giving and receiving feedback about skill performance, and completing skill homework assignments; see the Parent Orientation Note in Figure 14). Orienting parents to the types of skills and procedures used is necessary because many of the skill-use situations occur in the family environment. If parents are uninformed about Skillstreaming goals,

Figure 14   **Parent Orientation Note**

Date 12/20/02

Dear Parent or Guardian:

Your child and his or her classmates are learning to handle a variety of day-to-day concerns in positive ways. Sharing, taking turns, handling teasing and anger, and following directions are some of the concerns we are working on. We are all learning specific steps to social skills in order to handle these problems in acceptable ways.

The process we are using to learn these skills is called Skillstreaming. First, your child is watching someone else use the skill. Then he or she will try out the skill and receive feedback about how well he or she performed the skill from both peers and adults. Finally, your child will be asked to practice the skill in real-life situations.

Each week we will be sending home a note describing the skill and its steps. We hope that you review the weekly skill sheet with your child and help your child practice the skill at home. Please feel free to call me at _____555-1234_____ if you have any questions.

Sincerely,

_____Teacher/Leader_____

they may justifiably question the purpose of discussing home-related situations at school.

Other ways to promote parent involvement at the orientation level include the following:

1. Have parents assess their child's skill strengths and weaknesses by completing all or part of the Parent Skillstreaming Checklist (presented in Appendix B), and talk with them about skills they value in the home. Conversations with parents about needed skills will help identify cultural aspects of the skills and permit better choices of where, when, and with whom individual skills will be most beneficial.

2. Frequently inform parents of the child's progress in the various skill areas, focusing on positive reports. (Parent Homework Notes, described in the following discussion, are the vehicle for communication.)

3. Videotape the child in a role-play situation, and share this videotape with the parents during conferences to encourage further understanding of Skillstreaming's goals and procedures.

4. Invite parents to participate in a mock Skillstreaming group in which the parents learn a skill through modeling, role-playing, feedback, and homework.

5. Encourage parents to support skill learning by giving the child positive feedback for practicing skills he or she has successfully role-played in the school environment.

Support Level

Following successful parent involvement at the orientation level, the teacher or other group leader should seek to involve parents at the support level. The goal at this level is to gain more active parental support. Parent activities at this level are as follows:

1. Supporting the child's demonstration of the social skill by helping the child complete assigned homework in the home environment. Feedback to the teacher will be given via the Homework Report forms (see Figures 2 and 3, on pages 64 and 66) or Parent Homework Notes (Figures 15 and 16).

Figure 15   **Parent Homework Note 1**

Student _____Natalie_____ Date _1/10/03_____

Dear Parent or Guardian:

This week we are working on the following skill:

_____Dealing with Mistakes (#33)_____

This is a very important skill for your child to learn. The steps of the skill are:

_____1. Say, "It's OK to make mistakes. Everybody makes mistakes."___

_____2. Plan for next time._____

_____

_____

_____

_____

Your child has completed a homework assignment on this skill. Please review this assignment with your child.

Please feel free to call if you have any questions.

Sincerely,

_____Teacher/Leader_____

FIGURE 16   **Parent Homework Note 2**

Student _____Thomas_____ Date _____1/15/03_____

Dear Parent or Guardian:

We are working on the following skill:

_____Accepting No (#39)_____

This is a very important skill for your child to learn. The steps of the skill are:

_____1. Stop and think._____

_____2. Choose._____

_____a. Do something else._____

_____b. Ask to talk._____

_____3. Do it._____

Your child has learned this skill well but will need continued practice. Please watch for the skill at home! If you see a situation when the skill could be used, please encourage your child to use this skill. Enclosed is a Parent Award to complete and return to school when you see your child use this skill.

Please feel free to call if you have any questions.

Sincerely,

_____Teacher/Leader_____

2. Noticing and rewarding specific skill use by the child in the home and neighborhood environment and providing ongoing encouragement by giving the child Parent Awards (see the sample in Figure 12, on page 178) to take home, then return to school

3. Being invited to and observing a Skillstreaming group in progress and participating as coactors in the group

4. Helping to assess the child's skill progress by judging skill performance at home and in neighborhood settings. The Skillstreaming in Early Childhood Rubric, given in Appendix C, may be used for this purpose

Cooperative Level

At the cooperative level, parents are involved in selecting skills needed in the home and neighborhood setting and regularly give feedback to the teacher or other group leader about the child's use of the Skillstreaming skills. Parent Homework Note 3 (Figure 17) is useful for structuring more direct parent involvement. Parents will also be involved in prompting the child's use of the skills at home and will provide encouragement and reinforcement for the child's performance (see the Skillstreaming Request to Parents, Figure 18). At the cooperative level, teachers and parents work together as a team to teach and support the child's skill development.

SUMMARY

Involving parents in the child's learning of prosocial skills has the potential to support the child in continued use of positive behaviors. When parents are successful prompting, coaching, and reinforcing skill use, their parenting skills and the child's social skills are enhanced. Although parent involvement is often challenging for teachers and others who work with young children, creating a partnership between home and school allows parents to learn more supportive parenting strategies and make greater and more lasting changes in the young child's social adjustment.

FIGURE 17 **Parent Homework Note 3**

Student _____Joleen_____ Date _1/23/03_

Dear Parent or Guardian:

Your child has been working on the following skill:

_____Dealing with Feeling Mad (#28)_____

This is a very important skill for your child to learn. The steps of the skill are:

_____1. Stop and think._____

_____2. Choose._____

_____a. Turtle._____

_____b. Relax._____

_____c. Ask to talk._____

_____3. Do it._____

Your child has been asked to complete this skill at home. Please help your child to follow these skill steps.

Please sign and return this form to _____Teacher/Leader_____ with your comments (on the back) about quality of homework done and any questions/suggestions by __1/27/03__.

Parent signature _____ Date __1/27/03__

FIGURE 18   Skillstreaming Request to Parents

Student _____Cory_____ Date ___10/27/02____

Dear Parent or Guardian:

Your child is working on the following skill(s):

_____Waiting Your Turn (#16)_____

_____Sharing (#17)_____

_____Offering Help (#18)_____

The steps to these skills are attached to this note. Please help your child practice at home by doing the following:

- Remind your child to use the skill when you see a time the skill could be helpful.
- Respond positively to your child's skill use (allow the skill use to be successful).
- Reward your child's use of the skill. (You may use a Parent Award and have your child return this to school.)
- Ask your child to teach you (or a brother or sister) the skill.
- Other ___Role-playing Skill 17 (Sharing) before his cousin's visit.___

Please write any comments on the back of this form about how your child is learning and practicing this skill at home.

Sincerely,

_____Teacher/Leader_____

APPENDIX A

Skillstreaming Research on Children and Adolescents: An Annotated Bibliography

This appendix references and briefly describes research and support materials related to Skillstreaming's use with children and adolescents. Although the majority of studies examining the effectiveness of Skillstreaming have involved adults and adolescents, a few have included younger age groups. The reader is referred to *Skillstreaming the Elementary School Child* (McGinnis & Goldstein, 1997) or *Skillstreaming the Adolescent* (Goldstein & McGinnis, 1997) for a comprehensive bibliography of materials concerning all age groups. Overall, investigations combine to support the effectiveness of Skillstreaming with diverse age groups. Continuing tests of Skillstreaming's efficacy—along with specific instructional and generalization-enhancing procedures to enhance its effectiveness—are necessary. However, on the basis of the evidence that does exist, we confidently recommend Skillstreaming's continued and expanded use with all age groups.

Cobb, F. M. (1973). *Acquisition and retention of cooperative behavior in young boys through instructions, modeling, and structured learning.* Unpublished doctoral dissertation, Syracuse University.

   Trainees: First-grade boys (N = 80)

   Skill(s): Cooperation

   Experimental design: (1) Skillstreaming for cooperation, (2) instructions plus modeling of cooperation, (3) instructions for cooperation, (4) attention control, (5) no-treatment control

   Results: Skillstreaming significantly > all other conditions on both immediate and delayed tests of cooperative behavior.

Epstein, M., & Cullinan, D. (1987). Effective social skills curricula for behavior-disordered students. *Pointer, 31,* 21–24.

   A comparative description of six social skills curricula for secondary and elementary behavior-disordered students.

Fleming, L. R. (1977). *Training aggressive and unassertive educable mentally retarded children for assertive behaviors, using three types of Structured Learning Therapy.* Unpublished doctoral dissertation, Syracuse University.

   Trainees: Mentally retarded children (N = 96)

   Skill(s): Assertiveness

   Experimental design: (1) Skillstreaming for assertiveness plus fear-coping training, (2) Skillstreaming for assertiveness plus anger-coping training, (3) Skillstreaming for assertiveness, (4) attention control by aggressive versus unassertive children

   Results: All three Skillstreaming groups significantly > controls on increase in assertiveness. No significant in vivo transfer effects.

Goldstein, A. P. (1995). Coordinated multitargeted skills training: The promotion of generalization enhancement. In W. O'Donohue & L. Krasner (Eds.), *Handbook of psychological skills training: Clinical techniques and applications.* Boston: Allyn and Bacon.

   An examination of the problem of generalization failure, which has plagued interventions of all kinds, including those oriented toward teaching prosocial skills. Reviews the content and research base of procedures for the enhancement of both setting generalization (transfer) and temporal generalization (maintenance) of newly learned skills.

Healy, J. A. (1979). *Structured Learning Therapy and the promotion of transfer of training through the employment of overlearning and stimulus variability.* Unpublished doctoral dissertation, Syracuse University.

> *Trainees:* Unassertive adolescents in regular junior high school (N = 84)
>
> *Skill(s):* Assertiveness
>
> *Experimental design:* A 3 × 2 plus control factorial design reflecting the presence versus absence of stimulus variability by three levels of overlearning, plus brief instructions control
>
> *Results:* Significant effect for overlearning, not for stimulus variability.

Hummel, J. (1979). *Session variability and skill content as transfer enhancers in Structured Learning training.* Unpublished doctoral dissertation, Syracuse University.

> *Trainees:* Aggressive preadolescents (N = 47)
>
> *Skill(s):* Self-control, negotiation
>
> *Experimental design:* Skillstreaming-variable conditions versus Skillstreaming-constant conditions by self-control skill versus negotiation skill versus both
>
> *Results:* Skillstreaming-variable conditions significantly > Skillstreaming-constant conditions on both acquisition and transfer dependent measures across both skills singly and combined.

Jennings, R. L., & Davis, C. G. (1977). Attraction-enhancing client behaviors: A Structured Learning approach for "Non Yavis, Jr." *Journal of Consulting and Clinical Psychology, 45,* 135–144.

> *Trainees:* Emotionally disturbed lower socioeconomic children and adolescents (N = 40)
>
> *Skill(s):* Interviewee behaviors (initiation, terminating silences, elaboration, and expression of affect)

Experimental design: (1) Skillstreaming for interviewee behaviors versus (2) minimal treatment control in a 2 × 2 × 4 factorial design reflecting (a) repeated measures, (b) treatments, and (c) interviewers

Results: Skillstreaming significantly > minimal treatment control on interview initiation and terminating silences. No significant effects on interview elaboration or expression of affect. Skillstreaming significantly > minimal treatment control on attractiveness to interviewer on portion of study measures.

Litwak, S. E. (1977). *The use of the helper therapy principle to increase therapeutic effectiveness and reduce therapeutic resistance: Structured Learning Therapy with resistant adolescents.* Unpublished doctoral dissertation, Syracuse University.

Trainees: Junior high school students (N = 48)

Skill(s): Following instructions

Experimental design: (1) Skillstreaming for following instructions—trainees anticipate serving as Skillstreaming trainers and (2) Skillstreaming for following instructions—no trainee anticipation of serving as trainers versus (3) no-treatment control by three parallel conditions involving a skill target not concerned with resistance reduction (i.e., expressing a compliment)

Results: Group 1 significantly > Group 2 significantly > Group 3 on both skills on immediate posttest and transfer measures.

McGinnis, E. (1985). Skillstreaming: Teaching social skills to children with behavioral disorders. *Teaching Exceptional Children, 17,* 160–167.

A description of the procedures, curriculum, and modifications in the Skillstreaming approach as applied to behavior disordered elementary-age children.

Miller, M. C. (1992). Student and teacher perceptions related to behavior change after Skillstreaming training. *Behavior Disorders, 17,* 271–295.

Trainees: Behavior-disordered adolescents (N = 70)

Skill(s): Several Skillstreaming skills

Experimental design: Pre-post comparisons of skill competence as perceived by trainees and by their teachers

Results: Substantial effects as a function of Skillstreaming as
rated by the trainees' teachers; absence of such effects in
trainees' own ratings.

Muris, P., Heldens, H., & Schreurs, L. (1992). Goldstein training for
children in special needs education. *Kind en Adolescent, 13,*
193–198.

A case study report of the impressionistically successful use
of Skillstreaming with four mentally retarded Dutch adolescents.

Reed, M. K. (1994). Social skills training to reduce depression in
adolescents. *Adolescence, 29,* 293–302.

Trainees: Seriously depressed adolescents (N = 10)

Skill(s): Social competency, self-evaluation, affective expression

Experimental design: Skillstreaming versus no-training control
plus male or female

Results: Both immediate and sustained reduction in depression for male trainees but not for females.

Sasso, G. M., Melloy, K. J., & Kavale, K. (1990). Generalization,
maintenance, and behavioral covariation associated with social
skills training through Structured Learning. *Behavioral Disorders,
16,* 9–22.

Three students with behavior disorders ranging in age from 8
to 13 years old participated in this study. All three were in a
self-contained special education classroom (training setting)
and were mainstreamed into at least one general education
class (generalization setting). Before, during, and after an 8-
week course of Skillstreaming, both they and three peers in
the regular class were observed across target skill behaviors.
All three trainees exhibited increases in three skill behaviors
in the training setting during the program. Two of the three
maintained these levels over a 10- to 20-week follow-up period

in the training setting and in the mainstream setting. The third did so for only one of the trained skills. Despite these successful outcome data, the prosocial behavior of all three subjects remained significantly below that of their peers in the regular class.

Stumphauzer, J. C. (1985). School programs: Staying in school and learning to learn. *Child and Youth Services, 8,* 137–146.

A review of delinquency prevention programs, including behavioral contracting, truancy control, parent training, vandalism reduction, school consultation, and Skillstreaming.

Swanstrom, C. R. (1978). *An examination of Structured Learning Therapy and the helper therapy principle in teaching a self-control strategy to school children with conduct problems.* Unpublished doctoral dissertation, Syracuse University.

Trainees: Elementary school children with acting-out problems (30 boys, 11 girls; N = 41)

Skill(s): Self-control

Experimental design: Skillstreaming versus structured discussion by helper experience versus helper structuring versus no helper role plus brief-instructions control

Results: Skillstreaming and structured discussion significantly > control on self-control acquisition. No significant transfer or helper role effects.

Skillstreaming Checklists and Grouping Chart

TEACHER/STAFF SKILLSTREAMING CHECKLIST

Student _____ Class/age _____

Teacher/staff _____ Date _____

INSTRUCTIONS: Listed below you will find a number of skills that children are more or less proficient in using. This checklist will help you evaluate how well each child uses the various skills. For each child, rate his/her use of each skill, based on your observations of his/her behavior in various situations.

Circle 1 if the child is *almost never* good at using the skill.

Circle 2 if the child is *seldom* good at using the skill.

Circle 3 if the child is *sometimes* good at using the skill.

Circle 4 if the child is *often* good at using the skill.

Circle 5 if the child is *almost always* good at using the skill.

Please rate the child on all skills listed. If you know of a situation in which the child has particular difficulty using the skill well, please note it briefly in the space marked "Problem situation."

	almost never	seldom	sometimes	often	almost always
1. **Listening:** Does the child appear to listen when someone is speaking and make an effort to understand what is said? Problem situation:	1	2	3	4	5
2. **Using Nice Talk:** Does the child speak to others in a friendly manner? Problem situation:	1	2	3	4	5
3. **Using Brave Talk:** Does the child use a brave or assertive tone of voice in a conflict with another child? Problem situation:	1	2	3	4	5

4. **Saying Thank You:** Does the child say thank you or in another way let others know he/she appreciates help given, favors, and so forth?

    1   2   3   4   5

Problem situation:

5. **Rewarding Yourself:** Does the child say when he/she has done a good job?

    1   2   3   4   5

Problem situation:

6. **Asking for Help:** Does the child request help when needed in an acceptable manner?

    1   2   3   4   5

Problem situation:

7. **Asking a Favor:** Does the child ask favors of others in an acceptable way?

    1   2   3   4   5

Problem situation:

8. **Ignoring:** Does the child ignore other children or situations when it is desirable to do so?

    1   2   3   4   5

Problem situation:

9. **Asking a Question:** Does the child ask questions about something he/she doesn't understand?

    1   2   3   4   5

Problem situation:

		almost never	seldom	sometimes	often	almost always

10. **Following Directions:** Does the child seem to understand directions and follow them? 1 2 3 4 5

Problem situation:

11. **Trying When It's Hard:** Does the child continue to try when something is difficult instead of giving up? 1 2 3 4 5

Problem situation:

12. **Interrupting:** Does the child interrupt when necessary in an appropriate manner? 1 2 3 4 5

Problem situation:

13. **Greeting Others:** Does the child acknowledge acquaintances when it is appropriate to do so? 1 2 3 4 5

Problem situation:

14. **Reading Others:** Does the child pay attention to a person's nonverbal language and seem to understand what is being communicated? 1 2 3 4 5

Problem situation:

15. **Joining In:** Does the child use acceptable ways of joining in an ongoing activity or group? 1 2 3 4 5

Problem situation:

	almost never	seldom	sometimes	often	almost always

16. **Waiting Your Turn:** Does the child wait his/her turn when playing a game with others?

    1   2   3   4   5

Problem situation:

17. **Sharing:** Does the child share most materials and toys with peers?

    1   2   3   4   5

Problem situation:

18. **Offering Help:** Does the child recognize when someone needs or wants help and offer assistance?

    1   2   3   4   5

Problem situation:

19. **Asking Someone to Play:** Does the child ask other children to play or extend an invitation to others to join in his/her activity?

    1   2   3   4   5

Problem situation:

20. **Playing a Game:** Does the child play games with peers in a fair manner?

    1   2   3   4   5

Problem situation:

21. **Knowing Your Feelings:** Does the child identify his/her feelings?

    1   2   3   4   5

Problem situation:

22. **Feeling Left Out:** Does the child deal with being left out of an activity without losing control or becoming upset?

       1   2   3   4   5

Problem situation:

23. **Asking to Talk:** Does the child verbally express when he/she seems upset?

       1   2   3   4   5

Problem situation:

24. **Dealing with Fear:** When afraid, does the child know why he/she is afraid and deal with this fear in an acceptable way (e.g., by talking about it)?

       1   2   3   4   5

Problem situation:

25. **Deciding How Someone Feels:** Does the child identify how another person appears to be feeling by what the person says?

       1   2   3   4   5

Problem situation:

26. **Showing Affection:** Does the child show that he/she likes someone in an acceptable way?

       1   2   3   4   5

Problem situation:

27. **Dealing with Teasing:** Does the child deal with being teased in acceptable ways?

    1   2   3   4   5

Problem situation:

28. **Dealing with Feeling Mad:** Does the child use acceptable ways to express his/her anger?

    1   2   3   4   5

Problem situation:

29. **Deciding If It's Fair:** Does the child accurately assess what is fair and unfair?

    1   2   3   4   5

Problem situation:

30. **Solving a Problem:** When a problem occurs, does the child state alternative, prosocial ways to solve the problem?

    1   2   3   4   5

Problem situation:

31. **Accepting Consequences:** Does the child accept the consequences for his/her behavior without becoming angry or upset?

    1   2   3   4   5

Problem situation:

32. **Relaxing:** Is the child able to relax when tense or upset?

    1   2   3   4   5

Problem situation:

33. **Dealing with Mistakes:** Does the child accept making mistakes without becoming upset?   1   2   3   4   5

Problem situation:

34. **Being Honest:** Is the child honest when confronted with a negative behavior?   1   2   3   4   5

Problem situation:

35. **Knowing When to Tell:** Does the child refrain from telling on others about small problems?   1   2   3   4   5

Problem situation:

36. **Dealing with Losing:** Does the child accept losing at a game or activity without becoming upset or angry?   1   2   3   4   5

Problem situation:

37. **Wanting to Be First:** Does the child accept not being first at a game or activity?   1   2   3   4   5

Problem situation:

38. **Saying No:** Does the child say no in an acceptable manner to things he/she doesn't want to do or to things that may get him/her into trouble?   1   2   3   4   5

Problem situation:

almost never   seldom   sometimes   often   almost always

39. **Accepting No:** Does the child accept   1   2   3   4   5
being told no without becoming
upset?

Problem situation:

40. **Deciding What to Do:** Does the child   1   2   3   4   5
choose acceptable activities on his/her
own when feeling bored?

Problem situation:

PARENT SKILLSTREAMING CHECKLIST

Name _____ Date _____

Child's name _____ Birth date _____

INSTRUCTIONS: Based on your observations in various situations, rate your child's use of the following skills.

> Circle 1 if the child is *almost never* good at using the skill.
> Circle 2 if the child is *seldom* good at using the skill.
> Circle 3 if the child is *sometimes* good at using the skill.
> Circle 4 if the child is *often* good at using the skill.
> Circle 5 if the child is *almost always* good at using the skill.

	almost never	seldom	sometimes	often	almost always
1. **Listening:** Does your child listen and understand when you or others talk to him/her? Comments:	1	2	3	4	5
2. **Using Nice Talk:** Does your child speak to others in a friendly manner? Comments:	1	2	3	4	5
3. **Using Brave Talk:** Does your child use a brave or assertive tone of voice in a conflict with another child? Comments:	1	2	3	4	5
4. **Saying Thank You:** Does your child say thank you or in another way show thanks when someone does something nice for him/her? Comments:	1	2	3	4	5

5. **Rewarding Yourself:** Does your child tell you when he/she has done a good job?

   1   2   3   4   5

Comments:

6. **Asking for Help:** Does your child ask in a friendly way when he/she needs help?

   1   2   3   4   5

Comments:

7. **Asking a Favor:** Does your child ask favors of others in an acceptable way?

   1   2   3   4   5

Comments:

8. **Ignoring:** Does your child ignore other children or situations when it is desirable to ignore them?

   1   2   3   4   5

Comments:

9. **Asking a Question:** Does your child ask questions about something he/she doesn't understand?

   1   2   3   4   5

Comments:

10. **Following Directions:** Does your child seem to understand and follow directions that you give?

   1   2   3   4   5

Comments:

	almost never	seldom	sometimes	often	almost always

11. **Trying When It's Hard:** Does your child continue to try when something is difficult instead of giving up?

    1   2   3   4   5

Comments:

12. **Interrupting:** Does your child know when and how to interrupt when he/she needs something?

    1   2   3   4   5

Comments:

13. **Greeting Others:** Does your child acknowledge acquaintances when it is appropriate to do so?

    1   2   3   4   5

Comments:

14. **Reading Others:** Does your child pay attention to a person's nonverbal language and seem to understand what is being communicated?

    1   2   3   4   5

Comments:

15. **Joining In:** Does your child use acceptable ways of joining in an activity with friends or family?

    1   2   3   4   5

Comments:

16. **Waiting Your Turn:** Does your child wait his/her turn when playing a game with others?

    1   2   3   4   5

Comments:

17. **Sharing:** Does your child share most materials and toys with his/her friends?

    1   2   3   4   5

Comments:

18. **Offering Help:** Does your child recognize when someone needs or wants help and offer this help?

    1   2   3   4   5

Comments:

19. **Asking Someone to Play:** Does your child ask other children to play or join in his/her activity?

    1   2   3   4   5

Comments:

20. **Playing a Game:** Does your child play games with friends in a fair manner?

    1   2   3   4   5

Comments:

21. **Knowing Your Feelings:** Does your child identify his/her feelings?

    1   2   3   4   5

Comments:

22. **Feeling Left Out:** Does your child deal with being left out of an activity without losing control or becoming upset?

    1   2   3   4   5

Comments:

almost never seldom sometimes often almost always

23. **Asking to Talk:** Does your child talk about his/her problems when upset?   1 2 3 4 5

Comments:

24. **Dealing with Fear:** Does your child know why he/she is afraid and deal with this fear in an acceptable way (e.g., by talking about it)?   1 2 3 4 5

Comments:

25. **Deciding How Someone Feels:** Does your child identify how another person appears to be feeling by what the person says?   1 2 3 4 5

Comments:

26. **Showing Affection:** Does your child show that he/she likes someone in an acceptable way?   1 2 3 4 5

Comments:

27. **Dealing with Teasing:** Does your child deal with being teased in acceptable ways?   1 2 3 4 5

Comments:

28. **Dealing with Feeling Mad:** Does your child use acceptable ways to express his/her anger?   1 2 3 4 5

Comments:

	almost never	seldom	sometimes	often	almost always

29. **Deciding If It's Fair:** Does your child accurately assess what is fair and unfair?   1   2   3   4   5

Comments:

30. **Solving a Problem:** When a problem occurs, does your child state alternative, acceptable ways to solve the problem?   1   2   3   4   5

Comments:

31. **Accepting Consequences:** Does your child accept the consequences for his/her behavior without becoming angry or upset?   1   2   3   4   5

Comments:

32. **Relaxing:** Is your child able to relax when tense or upset?   1   2   3   4   5

Comments:

33. **Dealing with Mistakes:** Does your child accept making mistakes without becoming upset?   1   2   3   4   5

Comments:

34. **Being Honest:** Does your child admit that he/she has done something wrong when confronted?   1   2   3   4   5

Comments:

35. **Knowing When to Tell:** Does your child refrain from telling on others about small problems?   1 2 3 4 5

Comments:

36. **Dealing with Losing:** Does your child accept losing at a game or activity without becoming upset or angry?   1 2 3 4 5

Comments:

37. **Wanting to Be First:** Does your child accept not being first at a game or activity?   1 2 3 4 5

Comments:

38. **Saying No:** Does your child say no in an acceptable way to things he/she doesn't want to do or to things that may get him/her into trouble?   1 2 3 4 5

Comments:

39. **Accepting No:** Does your child accept being told no without becoming upset?   1 2 3 4 5

Comments:

40. **Deciding What to Do:** Does your child choose acceptable activities on his/her own when feeling bored?   1 2 3 4 5

Comments:

CHILD SKILLSTREAMING CHECKLIST

INSTRUCTIONS: Ask the child to point to the picture on the Child Skillstreaming Response Record corresponding to each question (rabbit, teddy bear, cat, etc.), listen carefully as you read the question, then color the face that shows how he/she feels. Repeat each question at least once.

SESSION 1

1. **Skill 1/rabbit:** Is it easy for you to listen and understand when someone is talking to you?

2. **Skill 2/teddy bear:** Is it easy for you to talk to others in a friendly way?

3. **Skill 3/cat:** Do you tell a person to stop when that person is bothering you without getting upset or mad?

4. **Skill 4/owl:** Do you say thank you or show thanks when someone has said or done something nice for you?

5. **Skill 5/elephant:** Do you tell about things that you do a good job with?

6. **Skill 6/flower:** Is it easy for you to ask in a friendly way when you need help?

7. **Skill 7/pig:** Is it easy for you to ask a favor of someone else?

8. **Skill 8/mouse:** Do you ignore others when they are acting silly?

9. **Skill 9/dog:** Do you ask questions about things you don't understand?

10. **Skill 10/bird:** Do you know what to do when directions are given?

SESSION 2

1. **Skill 11/rabbit:** Do you keep trying when something is hard to do?

2. **Skill 12/teddy bear:** When you want or need something from a teacher or parent who is busy, do you interrupt in a nice way?

3. **Skill 13/cat:** When you walk by somebody you know a little bit, do you smile and say hi?

4. **Skill 14/owl:** Can you tell when someone is sad or mad by how the person looks?

5. **Skill 15/elephant:** Is it easy for you to join in a game if you want to play?

6. **Skill 16/flower:** Is it easy for you to wait your turn when playing a game?

7. **Skill 17/pig:** Is it easy for you to share toys with friends?

8. **Skill 18/mouse:** Do you notice when someone needs or wants help and try to help the person?

9. **Skill 19/dog:** Is it easy for you to ask a friend to play?

10. **Skill 20/bird:** When playing a game, do you play fair?

SESSION 3

1. **Skill 21/rabbit:** Is it easy for you to say how you feel (mad, happy, frustrated)?

2. **Skill 22/teddy bear:** Do you still feel OK if you are left out of a game or activity?

3. **Skill 23/cat:** When you feel upset, is it easy for you to talk about why you're upset?

4. **Skill 24/owl:** When you feel afraid, do you talk to somebody about it?

5. **Skill 25/elephant:** Can you tell if somebody else is feeling mad, sad, or afraid by what the person says?

6. **Skill 26/flower:** Is it easy for you to show the people you like that you like them?

7. **Skill 27/pig:** When somebody teases you, can you keep from being upset?

8. **Skill 28/mouse:** Is it easy for you to stay in control when you are mad?

9. **Skill 29/dog:** Can you tell what is fair or not fair?

10. **Skill 30/bird:** If a problem happens, can you think of different ways to handle it—ways that won't get you into trouble?

1. **Skill 31/rabbit:** Do you accept your punishment when you've done something wrong without getting mad or upset?

2. **Skill 32/teddy bear:** When you feel tense or upset, is it easy for you to calm down?

3. **Skill 33/cat:** When you make a mistake on an activity or in a game, do you still feel OK?

4. **Skill 34/owl:** Do you tell the truth if you have done something wrong?

5. **Skill 35/elephant:** Can you keep from telling on someone else who does something wrong?

6. **Skill 36/flower:** If you lose at a game, can you keep from becoming upset or angry?

7. **Skill 37/pig:** Do you still feel OK if you are not first at a game or activity?

8. **Skill 38/mouse:** Is it easy to say no to something a friend wants you to do that you don't want to do or that might get you into trouble?

9. **Skill 39/dog:** When you are told no to something you want to do, can you keep from becoming upset?

10. **Skill 40/bird:** When you feel bored, can you choose something to do?

CHILD SKILLSTREAMING RESPONSE RECORD

Name _____ Birth date _____

School/program _____

Teacher/evaluator _____ Assessment date _____

1.

2.

3.

4.

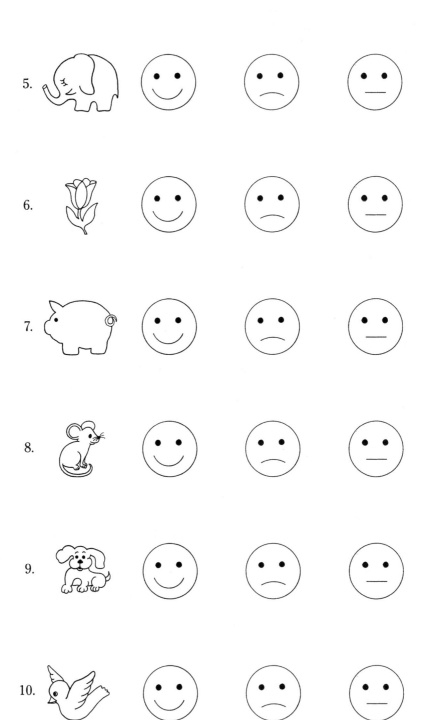

SKILLSTREAMING GROUPING CHART

	student names								
GROUP I: Beginning Social Skills									
1. Listening									
2. Using Nice Talk									
3. Using Brave Talk									
4. Saying Thank You									
5. Rewarding Yourself									
6. Asking for Help									
7. Asking a Favor									
8. Ignoring									
GROUP II: School-Related Skills									
9. Asking a Question									
10. Following Directions									
11. Trying When It's Hard									
12. Interrupting									
GROUP III: Friendship-Making Skills									
13. Greeting Others									
14. Reading Others									
15. Joining In									
16. Waiting Your Turn									
17. Sharing									
18. Offering Help									
19. Asking Someone to Play									
20. Playing a Game									

	student names									
GROUP IV: Dealing with Feelings										
21. Knowing Your Feelings										
22. Feeling Left Out										
23. Asking to Talk										
24. Dealing with Fear										
25. Deciding How Someone Feels										
26. Showing Affection										
GROUP V: Alternatives to Aggression										
27. Dealing with Teasing										
28. Dealing with Feeling Mad										
29. Deciding If It's Fair										
30. Solving a Problem										
31. Accepting Consequences										
GROUP VI: Dealing with Stress										
32. Relaxing										
33. Dealing with Mistakes										
34. Being Honest										
35. Knowing When to Tell										
36. Dealing with Losing										
37. Wanting to Be First										
38. Saying No										
39. Accepting No										
40. Deciding What to Do										

Skillstreaming in Early Childhood Rubric

Student name _____ Date _____

Evaluator name _____ Position _____

DIRECTIONS: Circle the number corresponding to your best assessment of the child's skills. Pre- and post-assessment may be completed by circling the number corresponding to skill proficiency in different colors. The specific area of concern (i.e., Academic, Peer Relations, Self-Control, Assertion, or Cooperation) may be circled or highlighted to indicate problematic situations and areas for instruction.

A. Listens (Academic; Cooperation; Peer Relations).

 4. Consistently and actively listens to others in almost all academic and behavioral group situations and seems to understand what is said.

 3. Consistently listens to others in most academic and behavioral situations and most of the time seems to understand what is being said.

 2. Sporadically demonstrates listening and understanding in some group and individual academic and behavioral situations.

 1. Rarely, if ever, demonstrates listening behaviors in any situation or setting.

Skills for instruction: Skill 1 (Listening)

Skill 8 (Ignoring)

B. Speaks to others in friendly or assertive ways (Academic; Peer Relations).

4. Consistently speaks to others in friendly or assertive ways appropriate to the social or academic situation.

3. Most of the time speaks to others in friendly or assertive ways appropriate to the social or academic situation.

2. Sporadically is able to speak to others in friendly or assertive ways in some social or academic situations.

1. Rarely, if ever, is able to speak to others appropriately in social or academic situations.

Skills for instruction: Skill 2 (Using Nice Talk)

Skill 3 (Using Brave Talk)

Skill 14 (Reading Others)

C. Asks for help or favors when needed (Academic; Assertion; Peer Relations).

4. Consistently asks for help or favors in appropriate ways whenever needed in academic and social situations.

3. Most of the time asks for help or favors in appropriate ways when needed in most academic and social situations.

2. Sporadically asks for help or favors in appropriate ways when needed in some academic and social situations.

1. Rarely, if ever, asks for help or favors appropriately when needed.

Skills for instruction: Skill 6 (Asking for Help)

Skill 7 (Asking a Favor)

Skill 23 (Asking to Talk)

D. Expresses appreciation (Academic; Peer Relations).

4. Consistently thanks others for help or favors given in appropriate ways in almost all academic and social situations.

3. Most of the time thanks others for help or favors given in appropriate ways in most academic and social situations.

2. Occasionally thanks others for help or favors given in appropriate ways in some academic and social situations.

1. Rarely, if ever, thanks others appropriately for help or favors given in either academic or social situations.

Skill for instruction: Skill 4 (Saying Thank You)

E. Evaluates own performance (Academic; Self-Control; Assertion).

4. Consistently and accurately identifies and rewards self for a job well done.

3. Most of the time identifies when a job is well done and rewards self appropriately.

2. Occasionally identifies when a job is well done and rewards self appropriately.

1. Rarely, if ever, identifies when a job is well done and rewards self appropriately.

Skill for instruction: Skill 5 (Rewarding Yourself)

F. Avoids problematic or conflict situations by ignoring (Peer Relations; Academic; Self-Control; Cooperation).

4. Consistently ignores distracting or problematic peer behavior in academic and social situations when it is appropriate to do so.

3. Most of the time ignores distracting or problematic peer behavior in most academic and social situations when it is appropriate to do so.

2. Occasionally ignores distracting or problematic peer behavior in some academic and social situations when it is appropriate to do so.

1. Rarely, if ever, ignores distracting or problematic peer behavior in any situation.

Skills for instruction: Skill 8 (Ignoring)

Skill 35 (Knowing When to Tell)

G. Follows directions and completes tasks (Academic; Self-Control; Cooperation).

   4. Consistently follows directions in almost all academic and cooperative situations, asking questions to clarify and following through to the completion of the task or direction.

   3. Most of the time follows directions in most academic and cooperative situations, asking questions to clarify and following through to the completion of the task or direction.

   2. Occasionally follows directions in some academic and cooperative situations, at times asking questions to clarify and occasionally following through to the completion of the task or direction.

   1. Rarely, if ever, follows directions, asks clarifying questions, or completes tasks.

   Skills for instruction: Skill 9 (Asking a Question)

   Skill 10 (Following Directions)

   Skill 11 (Trying When It's Hard)

H. Interrupts appropriately and under appropriate circumstances (Self-Control; Academic; Assertion).

   4. Consistently interrupts others appropriately when necessary in social and academic situations.

   3. Most of the time interrupts others appropriately when necessary in social and academic situations.

   2. Occasionally interrupts others appropriately when necessary in social and academic situations.

   1. Rarely, if ever, interrupts in an appropriate manner.

   Skills for instruction: Skill 12 (Interrupting)

   Skill 35 (Knowing When to Tell)

I. Initiates contacts with others (Peer Relations; Assertion).

   4. Consistently and actively acknowledges others and joins in activities in the classroom or with peers in an appropriate and natural manner.

3. Most of the time acknowledges others and joins in activities in the classroom or with peers in an appropriate and natural manner.

2. Occasionally acknowledges others and sometimes joins in activities in the classroom or with peers in a somewhat appropriate manner.

1. Rarely, if ever, initiates interaction with others in an appropriate manner.

Skills for instruction: Skill 13 (Greeting Others)

Skill 15 (Joining In)

Skill 19 (Asking Someone to Play)

J. Is sensitive to nonverbal communication (Peer Relations; Self-Control).

4. Consistently demonstrates understanding of and insight about the nonverbal communication of others in almost all situations.

3. Most of the time demonstrates understanding of and insight about the nonverbal communication of others in most situations.

2. Occasionally demonstrates understanding of and insight about the nonverbal communication of others in some situations.

1. Rarely, if ever, demonstrates understanding and insight, misreading others' nonverbal communication.

Skills for instruction: Skill 14 (Reading Others)

Skill 25 (Deciding How Someone Feels)

Skill 28 (Dealing with Feeling Mad)

K. Plays appropriately with others (Academic; Peer Relations; Self-Control; Assertion; Cooperation).

4. Consistently and actively cooperates with others during almost all academic or social games.

3. Most of the time cooperates with others during academic or social games.

2. Occasionally cooperates with others during academic or social games.

1. Rarely, if ever, cooperates with others during academic or social games.

Skills for instruction: Skill 16 (Waiting Your Turn)

Skill 17 (Sharing)

Skill 20 (Playing a Game)

Skill 36 (Dealing with Losing)

Skill 37 (Wanting to Be First)

L. Understands the feelings of others (Peer Relations; Cooperation; Self-Control).

4. Consistently and actively seeks to understand the feelings of another in almost all appropriate situations when that person is experiencing a problem.

3. Most of the time actively seeks to understand the feelings of another in most appropriate situations when that person is experiencing a problem.

2. Occasionally seeks to understand the feelings of another in most appropriate situations when that person is experiencing a problem.

1. Rarely, if ever, notices or seeks to understand the feelings of another.

Skill for instruction: Skill 25 (Deciding How Someone Feels)

M. Demonstrates empathy (Peer Relations; Cooperation).

4. Consistently and actively demonstrates empathy toward another when that person is upset or sad.

3. Most of the time demonstrates empathy toward another when that person is upset or sad.

2. Occasionally demonstrates empathy toward another when that person is upset or sad.

1. Rarely, if ever, demonstrates empathy toward another.

Skills for instruction: Skill 18 (Offering Help)

Skill 26 (Showing Affection)

N. Identifies own feelings (Self-Control).

    4. Consistently identifies own feelings in appropriate situations.

    3. Most of the time identifies own feelings in appropriate situations.

    2. Occasionally identifies own feelings in appropriate situations.

    1. Rarely, if ever, identifies own feelings.

    Skill for instruction: Skill 21 (Knowing Your Feelings)

O. Identifies feelings appropriate to a situation (Assertion; Peer Relations; Academic; Self-Control).

    4. Consistently interprets situations accurately and identifies appropriate feelings.

    3. Most of the time interprets situations accurately and identifies appropriate feelings.

    2. Occasionally interprets situations accurately and identifies appropriate feelings.

    1. Rarely, if ever, interprets situations accurately and identifies appropriate feelings.

    Skills for instruction: Skill 11 (Trying When It's Hard)
                               Skill 14 (Reading Others)
                               Skill 21 (Knowing Your Feelings)
                               Skill 22 (Feeling Left Out)
                               Skill 24 (Dealing with Fear)
                               Skill 28 (Dealing with Feeling Mad)
                               Skill 33 (Dealing with Mistakes)
                               Skill 36 (Dealing with Losing)

P. Shows affection (Peer Relations; Cooperation).

    4. Consistently displays affection appropriate to the person and in appropriate ways when it is relevant to do so.

    3. Most of the time displays affection appropriate to the person and in appropriate ways when it is relevant to do so.

2. Occasionally displays affection appropriate to the person and in appropriate ways when it is relevant to do so.

1. Rarely, if ever, displays affection appropriately when it is relevant to do so.

Skill for instruction: Skill 26 (Showing Affection)

Q. Deals with anger and conflict (Self-Control; Peer Relations; Cooperation).

4. Consistently deals with anger and conflict appropriately in almost all situations.

3. Most of the time deals with anger and conflict appropriately in most situations.

2. Occasionally deals with anger and conflict appropriately in some situations.

1. Rarely, if ever, deals with anger and conflict appropriately in any situation.

Skills for instruction: Skill 23 (Asking to Talk)

Skill 28 (Dealing with Feeling Mad)

Skill 30 (Solving a Problem)

Skill 31 (Accepting Consequences)

Skill 32 (Relaxing)

Skill 33 (Dealing with Mistakes)

Skill 39 (Accepting No)

R. Deals with peer provocation (Self-Control; Peer Relations).

4. Consistently deals with peer provocation in productive ways.

3. Most of the time deals with peer provocation in productive ways.

2. Occasionally deals with peer provocation in productive ways.

1. Rarely, if ever, deals with peer provocation in productive ways.

Skills for instruction: Skill 23 (Asking to Talk)

Skill 27 (Dealing with Teasing)

Skill 35 (Knowing When to Tell)

S. Decides what is fair (Self-Control; Peer Relations).

4. Consistently and accurately assesses what is fair and unfair in almost all situations when appropriate.

3. Most of the time accurately assesses what is fair and unfair in most situations when appropriate.

2. Occasionally accurately assesses what is fair and unfair in some situations when appropriate.

1. Rarely, if ever, accurately assesses what is fair and unfair.

Skill for instruction: Skill 29 (Deciding If It's Fair)

T. Accepts consequences (Self-Control; Cooperation; Academic).

4. Consistently accepts consequences of own actions appropriately in almost all situations.

3. Most of the time accepts consequences of own actions appropriately in most situations.

2. Occasionally accepts consequences of own actions appropriately in some situations.

1. Rarely, if ever, accepts consequences of own actions appropriately.

Skills for instruction: Skill 31 (Accepting Consequences)

Skill 32 (Relaxing)

Skill 33 (Dealing with Mistakes)

Skill 34 (Being Honest)

U. Resists peer pressure (Cooperation; Peer Relations; Self-Control).

4. Consistently says no in an acceptable manner to things he/she doesn't want to do or to things that may be trouble.

3. Most of the time says no in an acceptable manner to things he/she doesn't want to do or to things that may be trouble.

2. Occasionally says no in an acceptable manner to things he/she doesn't want to do or to things that may be trouble.

1. Rarely, if ever, says no in an acceptable manner to things he/she doesn't want to do or to things that may be trouble.

Skills for instruction: Skill 29 (Deciding If It's Fair)

Skill 30 (Solving a Problem)

Skill 38 (Saying No)

V. Accepts being told no (Cooperation; Peer Relations; Self-Control).

4. Consistently accepts being told no in an acceptable way.

3. Most of the time accepts being told no in an acceptable way.

2. Occasionally accepts being told no in an acceptable way.

1. Rarely, if ever, accepts being told no in an acceptable way.

Skill for instruction: Skill 39 (Accepting No)

W. Uses free time appropriately (Cooperation; Assertion).

4. Consistently selects acceptable activities when feeling bored.

3. Most of the time selects acceptable activities when feeling bored.

2. Occasionally selects acceptable activities when feeling bored.

1. Rarely, if ever, selects acceptable activities when feeling bored.

Skill for instruction: Skill 40 (Deciding What to Do)

Supplementary Skillstreaming Components

All that is truly needed to implement a Skillstreaming program for preschool and kindergarten children is this program text. However, other Skillstreaming materials, both print and video, will make the task easier. Supplementary Skillstreaming components for preschool and kindergarten children are described in this appendix. Skillstreaming components for elementary-age children and adolescents are listed in Appendix E.

For current prices and ordering information, write, call, fax, or visit our Web site:

Research Press
2612 North Mattis Avenue
Champaign, Illinois 61822
Phone: (217) 352–3273
Toll-Free: (800) 519–2707
Fax: (217) 352–1221
Web site: www.researchpress.com

Print Components

Program Forms

Skillstreaming in Early Childhood: New Strategies and Perspectives for Teaching Prosocial Skills—Program Forms, by Dr. Ellen McGinnis and Dr. Arnold P. Goldstein, 2003 (papercover, 8½ × 11–inch format, 52 pages, ISBN 0–87822–475–0).

CONTENTS

- Teacher/Staff, Parent, and Child Skillstreaming Checklists
- Child Skillstreaming Response Record
- Skillstreaming Grouping Chart
- Skillstreaming in Early Childhood Rubric
- Homework Reports
- Self-Monitoring Forms
- Group Reward Forms
- Skill Tickets
- Skill Notes
- Teacher, Principal, and Parent Awards
- Goal-Setting Awards
- Parent Awards and Orientation and Homework Notes

Skill Cards

Skillstreaming in Early Childhood—Skill Cards, by Dr. Ellen McGinnis and Dr. Arnold P. Goldstein, 2003 (ISBN 0–87822–488–2).

Convenient 3 × 5–inch cards designed for student use during Skillstreaming sessions and homework assignments. Cards list the behavioral steps for each of the 40 early childhood and kindergarten Skillstreaming skills. Eight cards are provided for each skill (320 cards in all).

Video Component

The Skillstreaming Video: How to Teach Students Prosocial Skills, by Dr. Arnold P. Goldstein and Dr. Ellen McGinnis, 1988 (ISBN 0–87822–389–4; 26 minutes).

Designed for teachers and other staff, this videotape shows Drs. Goldstein and McGinnis in actual training sessions with educators and small groups of adolescents and elementary-age children. Clearly demonstrates the Skillstreaming teaching model and the program's four major components—modeling, role-playing, performance feedback, and generalization.

Skillstreaming Materials for Other Instructional Levels

Elementary-Age Children

Program Text

Skillstreaming the Elementary School Child: New Strategies and Perspectives for Teaching Prosocial Skills (Rev. ed.), by Dr. Ellen McGinnis and Dr. Arnold P. Goldstein, 1997 (papercover, 352 pages, ISBN 0–87822–372–X).

Program Forms

Skillstreaming the Elementary School Child: New Strategies and Perspectives for Teaching Prosocial Skills—Program Forms (Rev. ed.), by Dr. Ellen McGinnis and Dr. Arnold P. Goldstein, 1997 (papercover, 8½ × 11–inch format, 64 pages, ISBN 0–87822–374–6).

Student Manual

Skillstreaming the Elementary School Child—Student Manual, by Dr. Ellen McGinnis and Dr. Arnold P. Goldstein, 1997 (papercover, 8½ × 11–inch format, 80 pages, ISBN 0–87822–373–8).

Student Video

People Skills: Doing 'em Right! (Elementary Level), by
Dr. Ellen McGinnis and Dr. Arnold P. Goldstein, 1997
(ISBN 0–87822–385–1; 17 minutes).

Skill Cards

Skillstreaming the Elementary School Child—Skill Cards,
by Dr. Ellen McGinnis and Dr. Arnold P. Goldstein, 1997
(ISBN 0–87822–387–8).

Adolescents

Program Text

*Skillstreaming the Adolescent: New Strategies and Perspec-
tives for Teaching Prosocial Skills* (Rev. ed.), by Dr. Arnold P.
Goldstein and Dr. Ellen McGinnis (with R. P. Sprafkin, N. J.
Gershaw, and P. Klein), 1997 (papercover, 352 pages, ISBN
0–87822–369–X).

Program Forms

*Skillstreaming the Adolescent: New Strategies and Perspec-
tives for Teaching Prosocial Skills—Program Forms,* by Dr.
Arnold P. Goldstein and Dr. Ellen McGinnis, 1997 (papercover, 8½ × 11–inch format, 48 pages, ISBN 0–87822–371–1).

Student Manual

Skillstreaming the Adolescent—Student Manual, by Dr.
Arnold P. Goldstein and Dr. Ellen McGinnis, 1997 (papercover, 8½ × 11–inch format, 64 pages, ISBN 0–87822–370–3).

Student Video

People Skills: Doing 'em Right! (Adolescent Level), by
Dr. Arnold P. Goldstein and Dr. Ellen McGinnis, 1997
(ISBN 0–87822–386–X; 17 minutes).

Skill Cards

Skillstreaming the Adolescent—Skill Cards, by
Dr. Arnold P. Goldstein and Dr. Ellen McGinnis, 1997
(ISBN 0–87822–388–6).

Professional Training

*The Skillstreaming Video: How to Teach Students Prosocial
Skills,* by Dr. Arnold P. Goldstein and Dr. Ellen McGinnis,
1988 (ISBN 0–87822–389–4; 26 minutes).

REFERENCES

Ahmad, Y., & Smith, P. K. (1994). Bullying in schools and the issue of sex differences. In John Archer (Ed.), *Male violence*. London: Routledge.

Alberto, P. S., & Troutman, A. C. (1982). *Applied behavior analysis for teachers: Influencing student performance*. Columbus, OH: Charles E. Merrill.

Allen, K. E., & Marotz, L. R. (2000). *By the ages: Behavior and development of children pre-birth through eight*. Albany, NY: Delmar.

Ascher, C. (1994). *Gaining control of violence in the schools: A view from the field* (ERIC Digest No. 100). New York: ERIC Clearinghouse on Urban Education.

Atlas, R. S., & Pepler, D. J. (1998). Observations of bullying in the classroom. *Journal of Educational Research, 92,* 86–99.

Azrin, N. H., & Holz, W. C. (1966). Punishment. In W. K. Honig (Ed.), *Operant behavior: Areas of research and application*. New York: Appleton-Century-Crofts.

Bandura, A. (1973). *Aggression: A social learning analysis*. Englewood Cliffs, NJ: Prentice Hall.

Bandura, A. (1977). *Social learning theory*. Englewood Cliffs, NJ: Prentice Hall.

Banks, R. (1997). *Bullying in schools*. (ERIC Document Reproduction Service No. ED407154)

Beane, A. (1999). *The bully-free classroom*. Minneapolis: Free Spirit.

Bourland, E. (1995). *RRFC Links 2*(3). (Available from Federal Resource Center for Special Education, Academy for Educational Development, 1875 Connecticut Ave., NW, Washington, DC 20009–1202)

Brendtro, L. K., Brokenleg, M., & Van Bockern, S. (1998). *Reclaiming youth at risk: Our hope for the future*. Bloomington, IN: National Educational Service.

Buckley, N. K., & Walker, H. M. (1978). *Modifying classroom behavior: A manual of procedures for classroom teachers* (Rev. ed.). Champaign, IL: Research Press.

Buhremester, D. (1982). *Children's Concerns Inventory manual.* Los Angeles: University of California, Department of Psychiatry.

Camp, B. W., & Bash, M. A. S. (1981). *Think Aloud: Increasing social and cognitive skills—A problem-solving program for children* (Primary Level). Champaign, IL: Research Press.

Camp, B. W., & Bash, M. A. S. (1985). *Think Aloud: Increasing social and cognitive skills—A problem-solving program for children* (Classroom Program, Grades 1–2). Champaign, IL: Research Press.

Cartledge, G., & Feng, H. (1996). The relationship of culture and social behavior. In G. Cartledge with J. F. Milburn (Eds.), *Cultural diversity and social skills instruction: Understanding ethnic and gender differences.* Champaign, IL: Research Press.

Cartledge, G., & Johnson, S. (1997). Cultural sensitivity. In A. P. Goldstein & J. C. Conoley (Eds.), *School violence intervention: A practical handbook.* New York: Guilford.

Cartledge, G., & Milburn, J. F. (1980). *Teaching social skills to children.* New York: Pergamon.

Cartledge, G., & Milburn, J. F. (1995). *Teaching social skills to children and youth: Innovative approaches* (3rd ed.). Needham Heights, MA: Allyn and Bacon.

Cartledge, G., & Milburn, J. F. (1996). A model for teaching social skills. In G. Cartledge (Ed.), *Cultural diversity and social skills instruction: Understanding ethnic and gender differences.* Champaign, IL: Research Press.

Chan, K. S., & Rueda, R. (1979). Poverty and culture in education: Separate but equal. *Exceptional Children, 45,* 422–428.

Chapman, W. E. (1977). *Roots of character education.* Schenectady, NY: Character Research Press.

Coie, J. D., & Kupersmidt, J. B. (1983). A behavioral analysis of emerging social status in boys' groups. *Child Development, 54,* 1400–1416.

Cox, R. D., & Gunn, W. B. (1980). Interpersonal skills in the schools: Assessment and curriculum development. In D. P. Rathjen & J. P. Foreyt (Eds.), *Social competence: Interventions for children and adults.* New York: Pergamon.

Denham, S. A. (1998). *Emotional development in young children.* New York: Guilford.

Dewey, J. (1938). *Experience and education.* New York: Collier.

Dil, N. (1972). *Sensitivity of emotionally disturbed and emotionally non-disturbed elementary school children to emotional meanings of facial expressions.* Unpublished doctoral dissertation, Indiana University, Bloomington.

Dodge, K. A. (1983). Behavioral antecedents of peer social status. *Child Development, 54,* 1385–1399.

Dodge, K. A. (1985). Facets of social interaction and the assessment of social competence in children. In B. H. Schneider, K. H. Rubin, & J. E. Ledingham (Eds.), *Children's peer relations: Issues in assessment and intervention.* New York: Springer-Verlag.

Dodge, K. A., Coie, J. D., & Bralke, N. P. (1982). Behavior patterns of socially rejected and neglected preadolescents: The roles of social approach and aggression. *Journal of Abnormal Child Psychology, 10,* 389–410.

Dodge, K. A., Pettit, G. S., & Bates, J. E. (1994). Socialization mediators of the relation between socioeconomic status and child conduct problems. *Child Development, 65,* 649–665.

Dodge, K. A., Murphy, R. R., & Birchsbaum, K. C. (1984). The assessment of intention-cue detection skills in children: Implications for developmental psychology. *Child Development, 55,* 163–173.

Dodge, K. A., Schlundt, D. G., Schoken, I., & Dehugach, J. D. (1983). Social competence and children's sociometric status: The role of peer group entry strategies. *Merrill-Palmer Quarterly, 29,* 309–336.

Dreikurs, R., & Cassel, P. (1972). *Discipline without tears.* New York: Hawthorne.

Dreikurs, R., Grunwald, B., & Pepper, F. (1971). *Maintaining sanity in the classroom.* New York: Harper and Row.

Dryfoos, J. G. (1994). *Full-service schools.* San Francisco: Jossey-Bass.

Elliott, S. N., & Gresham, F. M. (1991). *Social skills intervention guide: Practical strategies for social skills training.* Circle Pines, MN: American Guidance Service.

Ellis, H. (1965). *The transfer of learning.* New York: Macmillan.

Emery, J. E. (1975). *Social perception processes in normal and learning disabled children.* Unpublished doctoral dissertation, New York University.

Epps, S., Thompson, F. J., & Lane, M. P. (1985). *Procedures for incorporating generalization programming into interventions for behaviorally disordered students.* Unpublished manuscript, Iowa State University, Ames.

Feindler, E. L. (1979). *Cognitive and behavioral approaches to anger control training in explosive adolescents.* Unpublished doctoral dissertation, West Virginia University, Morgantown.

Feindler, E. L., & Ecton, R. B. (1986). *Adolescent anger control: Cognitive-behavioral techniques.* New York: Pergamon.

Fialka, J., & Mikus, K. C. (1999). *Do you hear what I hear?* Ann Arbor, MI: Proctor.

Friesen, B. J., & Stephens, B. (1998). Expanding family roles in the system of care: Research and practice. In M. H. Epstein, K. Kutash, & A. Duchnowski (Eds.), *Outcomes for children and youth with behavioral and emotional disorders and their families.* Austin, TX: PRO-ED.

Gemelli, R. J. (1996). Understanding and helping children who do not talk in school. In N. J. Long & W. C. Morse (Eds.), *Conflict in the classroom: The education of at-risk and troubled students.* Austin, TX: PRO-ED.

Gibbs, J. C., Potter, G. B., & Goldstein, A. P. (1995). *The EQUIP program: Teaching youth to think and act responsibly through a peer-helping approach.* Champaign, IL: Research Press.

Golarz, R. J., & Golarz, M. J. (1995). *The power of participation: Improving schools in a democratic society.* Champaign, IL: Research Press.

Goldstein, A. P. (1999). *Low-level aggression: First steps on the ladder to violence.* Champaign, IL: Research Press.

Goldstein, A. P., Glick, B., & Gibbs, J. C. (1998). *Aggression replacement training: A comprehensive intervention for aggressive youth* (Rev. ed.). Champaign, IL: Research Press.

Goldstein, A. P., Glick, B., Irwin, J. J., Pask-McCartney, C., & Rubama, I. (1989). *Reducing delinquency: Intervention in the community.* New York: Pergamon.

Goldstein, A. P., Heller, K., & Sechrest, L. B. (1966). *Psychotherapy and the psychology of behavior change.* New York: Wiley.

Goldstein, A. P., & Kanfer, F. H. (1979). *Maximizing treatment gains.* New York: Academic.

Goldstein, A. P., & McGinnis, E. (1988). *The Skillstreaming video: How to teach students prosocial skills.* Champaign, IL: Research Press.

Goldstein, A. P., & McGinnis, E. (with R. P. Sprafkin, N. J. Gershaw, & P. Klein). (1997). *Skillstreaming the adolescent: New strategies and perspectives for teaching prosocial skills* (Rev. ed.). Champaign, IL: Research Press.

Goldstein, A. P., & Michaels, G. Y. (1985). *Empathy: Development, training and consequences.* Hillsdale, NJ: Erlbaum.

Goldstein, A. P., Palumbo, J., Striepling, S., & Voutsinas, A. M. (1995). *Break it up: A teacher's guide to managing student aggression.* Champaign, IL: Research Press.

Goleman, D. (1995). *Emotional intelligence.* New York: Bantam.

Graham, S., Harris, K. R., & Reid, R. (1992). Developing self-regulated learners. *Focus on Exceptional Children, 24,* 1–16.

Grant, S. H., & Van Acker, R. (2000). Do schools teach aggression? Recognizing and retooling the interactions that lead to aggression. *Reaching Today's Youth,* Fall, 27–32.

Grayson, M. C., Kiraly, J., Jr., & McKinnon, A. J. (1996). Using time-out procedures with disruptive students. In N. J. Long & W. C. Morse (Eds.), *Conflict in the classroom: The education of at-risk and troubled students.* Austin, TX: PRO-ED.

Greenbaum, S., Turner, B., & Stephens, R. D. (1989). *Set straight on bullies.* Malibu, CA: National School Safety Center.

Greenwood, C. R., Hops, H., Delquadri, J., & Guild, J. (1974). Group contingencies for group consequences in classroom management: A further analysis. *Journal of Applied Behavior Analysis, 7,* 413–425.

Greenwood, C. R., Todd, N. M., Hops, H., & Walker, H. M. (1978). *Description of withdrawn children's behavior in preschool settings* (Report No. 40). Eugene: University of Oregon, Center at Oregon for Research in the Behavioral Education of the Handicapped.

Greenwood, C. R., Todd, N. M., Hops, H., & Walker, H. M. (1982). Behavior change targets in the assessment and treatment of socially withdrawn preschool children. *Behavioral Assessment, 4,* 273–297.

Gresham, F. M. (1998). Social skills training: Should we raze, remodel, or rebuild? *Behavioral Disorders, 24*(1), 19–25.

Gresham, F. M., & Elliott, S. N. (1990). *Social Skills Rating System.* Circle Pines, MN: American Guidance Service.

Gresham, F. M., Sugai, G., & Horner, R. H. (2001). Interpreting outcomes of social skills training for students with high-incidence disabilities. *Exceptional Children, 67,* 331–344.

Guerra, N. J., & Slaby, R. G. (1989). Evaluative factors in social problem solving by aggressive boys. *Journal of Abnormal Child Psychology, 17,* 277–289.

Guzzetta, R. A. (1974). *Acquisition and transfer of empathy by the parents of early adolescents through Structured Learning training.* Unpublished doctoral dissertation, Syracuse University.

Hartup, W. W. (1983). Peer relations. In P. H. Mussen (Ed.), *Handbook of child psychology* (Vol. 4). New York: Wiley.

Hoover, J. H., & Oliver, R. (1996). *The bullying prevention handbook: A guide for principals, teachers, and counselors.* Bloomington, IN: National Education Service.

Jensen, E. (2000). *Brain-based learning.* San Diego: The Brain Store Publishing.

Jewett, J. (1992). *Aggression and cooperation: Helping young children develop constructive strategies.* (ERIC Document Reproduction Service No. ED351147)

Johnson, D. W., & Johnson, R. T. (1975). *Learning together and alone: Cooperation, competition, and individualization.* Englewood Cliffs, NJ: Prentice Hall.

Jolivette, K., Scott, T. M., & Nelson, C. M. (2000). *The link between Functional Behavioral Assessments (FBAs) and Behavioral Intervention Plans (BIPs)* (ERIC Digest E592). Reston, VA: Council for Exceptional Children.

Jones, V. F., & Jones, L. S. (1998). *Comprehensive classroom management* (5th ed.). Boston: Allyn and Bacon.

Kaplan, J. S., & Carter, J. (1995). *Beyond behavior modification: A cognitive behavioral approach to behavior management in the school* (3rd ed.). Austin, TX: PRO-ED.

Kauffman, J. M., Mostert, M. P., Trent, S. C., & Hallahan, D. P. (1998). *Managing classroom behavior: A reflective case-based approach* (2nd ed.). Boston: Allyn and Bacon.

Karoly, P., & Steffen, J. J. (1980). Operant methods. In F. H. Kanfer & A. P. Goldstein (Eds.), *Helping people change.* New York: Pergamon.

Kazdin, A. E. (1975). *Behavior modification in applied settings.* Homewood, IL: Dorsey.

Keeley, S. M., Shemberg, K. M., & Carbonell, J. (1976). Operant clinical intervention: Behavior management or beyond? Where are the data? *Behavior Therapy, 7,* 292–305.

Kendall, P. C., & Braswell, L. (1985). *Cognitive behavioral therapy for children.* New York: Guilford.

Keogh, B. K., & Burnstein, J. D. (1988). Relationship of temperament to preschoolers' interaction with peers and teachers. *Exceptional Children, 54,* 456–461.

Knight, B. J., & West, D. J. (1975). Temporary and continuing delinquency. *British Journal of Criminology, 15,* 43–50.

Kohlberg, L. (Ed.). (1973). *Collected papers on moral development and moral education.* Cambridge, MA: Harvard University, Center for Moral Education.

Kohn, A. (1986). *No contest.* Boston: Houghton Mifflin.

Kounin, J. (1970). *Discipline and group management in classrooms.* New York: Holt, Rinehart and Winston.

Kupersmidt, J. B. (1983, April). Predicting delinquency and academic problems from childhood peer status. In J. D. Coie (Chair), *Strategies for identifying children at social risk: Longitudinal correlates and consequences.* Symposium conducted at the biennial meeting of the Society for Research in Child Development, Detroit.

Ladd, G. W., Kochenderfer, B. J., & Coleman, C. C. (2000). Friendship and school adjustment: Friendship quality as a predictor of young children's early school adjustment. In W Craig (Ed.), *Childhood social development: The essential readings*. Malden, MS: Blackwell.

Ladd, G. W., & Mize, J. (1983). A cognitive-social learning model of social skill training. *Psychological Review, 90,* 127–157.

Lantieri, L. (1995). Waging peace in our schools: Beginning with the children. *Phi Delta Kappan, 76,* 386–388.

Little, V. L., & Kendall, P. C. (1979). Cognitive-behavioral interventions with delinquents: Problem solving, role-taking, and self-control. In P. C. Kendall & S. D. Hollon (Eds.), *Cognitive-behavioral interventions*. Orlando, FL: Academic.

Loeber, R., & Dishion, T. (1983). Early predictors of male delinquency: A review. *Psychological Bulletin, 94,* 68–99.

Luria, A. R. (1961). *The role of speech in the regulation of normal and abnormal behavior*. New York: Liveright.

Maccoby, E. E. (1980). *Social development*. New York: Harcourt Brace Jovanovich.

Manning, M., Heron, J., & Marshall, T. (1978). Styles of hostility and of social interactions at nursery, at school and at home: An extended study of children. In L. A. Hersov & M. Berger (Eds.), *Aggression and anti-social behavior in childhood and adolescence*. Oxford, UK: Pergamon.

Marzano, R. J., Pickering, D., & McTighe, J. (1993). *Assessing student outcomes: Performance assessment using the dimensions of learning model*. Alexandria, VA: Association for Supervision and Curriculum Development.

McGinnis, E., & Goldstein, A. P. (1990). *Skillstreaming in early childhood: Teaching prosocial skills to the preschool and kindergarten child*. Champaign, IL: Research Press.

McGinnis, E., & Goldstein, A. P. (1997). *Skillstreaming the elementary school child: New strategies and perpectives for teaching prosocial skills* (Rev. ed.). Champaign, IL: Research Press.

Meichenbaum, D. H. (1977). *Cognitive-behavior modification: An integrative approach*. New York: Plenum.

Miller, J. P. (1976). *Humanizing the classroom.* New York: Praeger.

Mize, J. (1995). Coaching preschool children in social skills: A cognitive social learning curriculum. In G. Cartledge & J. F. Milburn (Eds.), *Teaching social skills to children and youth: Innovative approaches* (3rd ed.). Needham Heights, MA: Allyn and Bacon.

Mize, J., & Ladd, G. W. (1984, April). Preschool children's goal and strategy knowledge: A comparison of picture-story and enactive assessment. In G. W. Ladd (Chair), *From preschool to high school: Are children's interpersonal goals and strategies predictive of their social competence?* Symposium conducted at the annual meeting of the American Educational Research Association, New Orleans.

Modro, M. (1995). *Safekeeping: Adult responsibility, children's right.* Providence: Behavioral Health Resource.

Morrison, R. L., & Bellack, A. S. (1981). The role of social perception in social skills. *Behavior Therapy, 12,* 69–70.

Natale, J. A. (1994, March). Roots of violence. *The American School Board Journal, 33–40.*

Neilans, T. H., & Israel, A. C. (1981). Towards maintenance and generalization of behavior change: Teaching children self-regulation and self-instructional skills. *Cognitive Therapy and Research, 5,* 189–196.

Nelson, J., Lott, L., & Glenn, H. S. (1993). *Positive discipline in the classroom: How to effectively use class meetings and other positive discipline strategies.* Rocklin, CA: Prima.

Newman, D. A., Horne, A. M., & Bartolomucci, C. L. (2000). *Bully busters: A teacher's manual for helping bullies, victims, and bystanders.* Champaign, IL: Research Press.

Nichols, P. (1996). *The curriculum of control: Twelve reasons for it, some arguments against it.* In N. C. Long & W. C. Morse (Eds.), *Conflict in the classroom.* Austin, TX: PRO-ED.

Olweus, D. (1991). Bully/victim problems among school children: Basic facts and effects of a school-based intervention program. In D. Pepler & K. H. Rubin (Eds.), *The development and treatment of childhood aggression.* Hillsdale, NJ: Erlbaum.

Olweus, D. (1993). *Bullying at school: What we know and what we can do.* Oxford, UK: Blackwell.

Osgood, C. E. (1953). *Method and theory in experimental psychology.* New York: Oxford University Press.

Patterson, G. R. (1982). *Coercive family process.* Eugene, OR: Castalia.

Patterson, G. R., Reid, J. B., Jones, R. R., & Conger, R. E. (1975). *A social learning approach to family intervention* (Vol. 1). Eugene, OR: Castalia.

Payne, R. (1998). *A framework for understanding poverty.* Baytown, TX: RFT Publishing.

Perry, P. G., Perry, L. C., & Rasmussen, P. (1986). Cognitive social learning mediators of aggression. *Child Development, 57,* 700–711.

Pettit, G. S., Bates, J. E., & Dodge, K. A. (2000). Supportive parenting, ecological context, and children's adjustment: A seven-year longitudinal study. In W. Craig (Ed.), *Childhood social development: The essential readings.* Malden, MS: Blackwell.

Piaget, J. (1962). *Play, dreams, and imitation in childhood.* New York: Norton.

Quinn, M. M., Osher, D., Warger, C. L., Hanley, T. V., Bader, B. D., & Hoffman, C. C. (2000). *Teaching and working with children who have emotional and behavioral challenges.* Longmont, CO: Sopris West.

Redl, F., & Wineman, D. (1957). *The aggressive child.* New York: Free Press.

Robins, L. N., West, P. A., & Herjanic, B. L. (1975). Arrests and delinquency in two generations: A study of black urban families and their children. *Journal of Child Psychology and Psychiatry, 16,* 125–140.

Rothenbert, B. B. (1970). Children's social sensitivity and the relationship to interpersonal competence, interpersonal comfort, and intellectual level. *Developmental Psychology, 2,* 335–350.

Sarason, I. G., Glaser, M., & Fargo, G. A. (1972). *Reinforcing productive classroom behavior.* New York: Behavioral Publications.

Sautter, R. C. (1995). Standing up to violence. *Phi Delta Kappan, 76,* K1–K12.

Schmoker, M. (1999). *Results: A key to continuous school improvement* (2nd ed.). Alexandria, VA: Association for Supervision and Curriculum Development.

Scott, T. M., & Nelson, C. M. (1998). Confusion and failure in facilitating generalized social responding in the school setting: Sometimes $2+2=5$. *Behavioral Disorders, 23*(4), 264–275.

Simon, S. G., Howe, L. W., & Kirschenbaum, H. (1972). *Values clarification.* New York: Hart.

Slavin, R. E. (1980). *Using student team learning* (Rev. ed.). Baltimore: Johns Hopkins University, Center for Social Organization of Schools.

Smith, P. K., & Levan, S. (1995). Perceptions and experiences of bullying in younger pupils. *British Journal of Educational Psychology, 65,* 489–500.

Spivack, G. E., & Shure, M. B. (1974). *Social adjustment of young children.* San Francisco: Jossey-Bass.

Stokes, T. F., & Baer, D. M. (1977). An implicit technology of generalization. *Journal of Applied Behavior Analysis, 10,* 349–367.

Strain, P. S., & Timm, M. A. (2001). Remediation and prevention of aggression: An evaluation of the regional intervention program over a quarter century. *Behavioral Disorders, 26*(4), 297–313.

Sulzer-Azaroff, B., & Mayer, G. R. (1991). *Behavior analysis for lasting change.* San Francisco: Holt, Rinehart and Winston.

Thorndike, E. L., & Woodworth, R. S. (1901). The influence of improvement in one mental function upon the efficiency of other functions. *Psychological Review, 8,* 247–261.

Walker, H. M. (1979). *The acting-out child: Coping with classroom disruption.* Boston: Allyn and Bacon.

Walker, H. M., Colvin, G., & Ramsey, E. (1995). *Antisocial behaviors in schools: Strategies and best practices.* Pacific Grove, CA: Brooks/Cole.

Werner, E. E., & Smith, R. S. (1982). *Vulnerable but invincible.* New York: McGraw-Hill.

Wilson, K. G., & Daviss, B. (1994). *Redesigning education.* New York: Holt.

Youth violence: A report of the Surgeon General (2001, January). Retrieved February 2, 2001, from http://www.surgeongeneral.gov/library/youthviolence/sgreport/toc.htm

Zahn-Waxler, C., & Radke-Yarrow, M. (1982). The development of altruism: Alternative research strategies. In N. Eisenberg (Ed.), *The development of prosocial behavior.* New York: Academic.

Zahn-Waxler, C., & Radke-Yarrow, M. (1990). The origins of empathic concern. *Motivation and Emotion, 14,* 107–130.

NAME INDEX

SUBJECT INDEX

Note: Numbers in boldface type denote pages listing skill steps and giving directions for teaching individual skills.

About the Authors

Ellen McGinnis earned her Ph.D. from the University of Iowa in 1986. She holds degrees in elementary education, special education, and school administration. She has been a teacher and an educational consultant in both public school settings and hospital-based programs and was an assistant professor of special education at the University of Wisconsin–Eau Claire. For the past 9 years, Dr. McGinnis served as principal of the education program at Orchard Place, a residential and day treatment facility for children and adolescents with emotional/behavioral disorders. She is currently Deputy Director of Student and Family Services for the Des Moines Public Schools. The author of numerous articles about identifying and teaching youth with emotional/behavioral disorders, Dr. McGinnis is coauthor, with Dr. Arnold P. Goldstein, of the revised editions of *Skillstreaming the Elementary School Child* and *Skillstreaming the Adolescent,* both published by Research Press. She and her husband, Carl Smith, are the parents of Sara, age 19, and Alex, age 15.

Arnold P. Goldstein (1933–2002) joined the clinical psychology section of Syracuse University's Psychology Department in 1963 and both taught there and directed its Psychotherapy Center until 1980. In 1981, he founded the university's Center for Research on Aggression. He joined Syracuse University's Division of Special Education in 1985 and in 1990 helped organize and codirect the New York State Taskforce on Juvenile Gangs. Dr. Goldstein had a career-long interest, as both researcher and practitioner, in difficult-to-reach clients. Since 1980, his main research and psychoeducational focus was youth violence. Dr. Goldstein's many books include, among others, *Delinquents on Delinquency, The Gang Intervention Handbook,* and the recently revised editions of *Skillstreaming the Adolescent, Aggression Replacement Training,* and *The Prepare Curriculum.* His most recent books are *Reducing Resistance* and *Lasting Change,* on the topics of managing resistance to therapy and promoting transfer and maintenance of gains, respectively. All of these titles are available from Research Press.